J. STANLEY MOORE

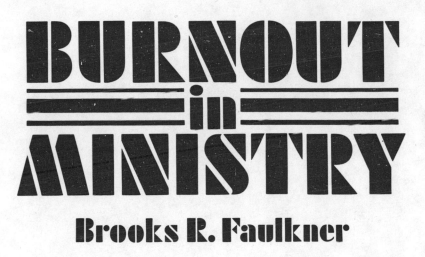

BURNOUT in MINISTRY

Brooks R. Faulkner

BROADMAN PRESS
Nashville, Tennessee

© Copyright 1981 • Broadman Press
All rights reserved.
4224-14
ISBN: 0-8054-2414-8

Dewey Decimal Classification: 253
Subject heading: MINISTERS
Library of Congress Catalog Card Number: 81-67752
Printed in the United States of America

Contents

Introduction

I had known him in seminary. He was bright and energetic. He was alive. He was competitive. He was one of those students that others matched their grades with.

It had been fifteen years since I had seen him. To say I was surprised by his statement was an understatement. I was stunned. He said, and with shocking candor, "I am burned out. I know I am only forty-one, but I am burned out. Last week the chairman of our deacons suggested I check out a counselor. He said that several of the deacons felt that I could no longer cut it. He's probably right. I just can't fake it anymore."

I had heard the story in similar ways before. For almost two decades, I have worked with ministers who were in some kind of dry spell. But his story was especially draining and discouraging. He was one of my heroes. He was one of those ministers with whom others measure their own effectiveness in ministry. I asked myself, *Is he burned out?*

Another close friend of mine is a minister of education. He called some weeks ago with quiet desperation in his voice. "I'm just not where I thought I would be when I graduated from seminary." "Where did you expect to be," I asked him. "I'm not sure. I just know I am not there."

Still another minister complained, "My friends seem to be finding fulfillment, and I just can't understand why I can't." How do you know that your friends are finding fulfillment, I asked him. "Well, they tell me that they are finding fulfillment. I have to take their word for it. Me . . . I'm in a rut."

A minister of youth was considering some options in what he wanted to do with the rest of his life. He was at that age where he had to decide if he was to work with youth for the rest of his ministry, or if he should take another turn vocationally. Not a new problem, but certainly a problem that gets more disturbing with age. The minister of youth was almost in panic in his search for solutions. This thirty-eight-year-old minister of youth told me, "I don't remember having this many problems with youth when I was a younger minister. It seems the parents have more to complain about than they did ten years ago. These parents want me to perform miracles with their youth. I just can't get as excited about working with youth as I used to." Was he burned out at thirty-eight?

"I don't think I have changed that much," said an Oklahoma minister of music, "but I am certain about one thing: the music has changed and when it did, I changed." He went on to share how his enthusiasm had waned with the passage of time. He had been in the church where he served for eleven years. He found it more and more difficult to find fulfillment in his work. The choir practices had become laborious. The solution of people problems were becoming more and more difficult. His work with the other staff problems was draining him of needed energy to work with his music program.

. . . What do these church leaders and ministers have in common? Consider the possibilities. . . . *What do the critics say they have in common?*

Some say they are not called in the first place . . .

If they were called, then certainly they would not be having the kind of serious vocational and personal problems they are having, these critics reason.

Although this reaction is common, it is so narrow in its definition that it is hard to take seriously, and too painful not to take seriously. The Pharisees are always with us. The superpious will always be there to make guilt waves for the people who hurt. This complaint should be heard because it is predictable that some will feel this way. One should try not to lose sleep over this first accusation toward the potential ministerial burnout. The Bible encourages us not to let the sun go down on our wrath. It is enough to be angry toward this judgement "only" temporarily . . . then consider it for what it is . . . duplicity (by definition, duplicity is "double dealing" or "deception by pretending to entertain one set of feelings and acting under the influence of another"). Such people want to accuse others of their own porblems. Being called does not make the minister immune to the problem of burnout.

Some say they should be heard, but not taken seriously . . .

It will pass like a headache. Burnout, these critics say, is a fad that will pass.

Well-intentioned persons are ubiquitous. They are everywhere. They are omnipresent. They suggest the ministers who complain of losing some of their "stuff" should not be taken seriously but rather they should be tolerated. Go ahead and hear them, they say, but know that it is a feeling that will pass.

Like ostriches, these well-intentioned persons bury their heads to the real problem. The minister who is facing difficult periods in his vocation should not be treated with the patronizing attitude of "Give them some time and they will pass through it." It is dehumanizing to him to have others treat him with lighthearted and patronizing tolerance. Persons with good intentions do little to help the struggling minister face tough vocational periods.

But others say they are facing potential burnout . . .
What do these ministers have in common? They are all facing a problem of the 1980s. They are facing ministerial burnout. They have run out of fuel. They are no less Christian. They are no less persons. They are simply facing a real problem which must be dealt with in a real way. To bury our heads and pretend it is not a reality is folly. Too many signals keep surfacing to deny it.

Burnout is not a problem isolated to the ministry. Every vocation with demands of professional expertise must face this problem. Major news magazines are filled with the stories of men and women who face burnout. Successful and effective persons who have spent their lives in preparation for their vocation leave their vocations suddenly and without explanation to pursue another. When describing what has happened to them, many describe signals of burnout.

This book centers on the problem of burnout in ministry. I have faced the problem personally. I expect to face the problem again in the last twenty-five years of my ministry. I believe that I have some handles to face this problem with determination and responsibility. I have spent the last fifteen years dealing with ministers who, like me, have faced, and are facing the problem of ministerial burnout. In a way, this book is a pilgrimage. Like John Bunyan, I hope there is progress in my pilgrimage. I am not writing in judgment of the minister who is facing the problem of burnout. I am writing in hope that, together, we can find ways to deal with it redemptively. I believe God is understanding. I believe that He knows that we must face the human problems which we help others through.

The intended audience of this book is ministers. These ministers include pastors, associate pastors, ministers of education, ministers of youth, combinations of both, ministers of music, age-group ministers, ministers of activities or recreation, church business administrators, denominational persons who are ministers, missionaries, and mavericks who minister in unpredictable but ingenious ways. It also includes those persons who teach ministers and/or affect the personal growth of ministers.

The secondary audience is any professional person who lives his or her life as a Christian with a commitment to serve Christ while living in a secular world.

A friend of mine was counseling with an adult male who was considering suicide. After a number of hours together, the adult male said to my friend, "I just don't feel any sense of hope. There is no light at the end of the tunnel."

In an effort to be helpful, my friend came up with a predictable homily. He said to the potential suicide, "Perhaps together we can find a candle which will help you find your way during this difficult time." Later, he said he remembered reading it somewhere . . . perhaps C. Roy Angell.

Amused at the simplicity of the homily, the adult male, an intelligent sort, smiled at the minister friend, "Pastor," he said, "is that the best you can do?"

My friend, now himself amused at his effort, replied, "What do you expect, a searchlight?" They laughed together. They had found the common thread of understanding. Afterwards, as the result of that little exchange, they became friends. They shared common problems. The potential suicide helped the pastor friend as much as the pastor friend helped the potential suicide. Actually they began to minister to each other.

In sharing the story of this exchange my friend was amazed at the fact that he had grown to trust this man who was troubled to the point of sharing his own pilgrimage struggle. He, himself, was facing burnout in his ministry. He was not as deeply troubled as the other man, but he was certainly not immune from some of the same exasperation that faced the potential suicide. They helped each other. Both found some help and some hope.

Although most of the readers of this book will not be potential suicides, some may be. Together perhaps we can find some hope and some help together. I know about potential burnout because of a personal pilgrimage. I have found some handles for myself. The anecdote above between the pastor and potential suicide is representative of my objective for this book. I want to explore some possibilities of facing burnout. You may be amused at some of my homilies. A candle, at very best, may be all I can offer. But after all, "What do you expect, a searchlight?"

Maybe we can help each other!

1
Burnout—the Closet Sin of Ministers

That we may be no longer children, tossed to and fro, and carried about with every wind of doctrine (Eph. 4:14a, ASV).

"I have been right zealous for the Eternal the God of hosts; the Israelites have forsaken thee, breaking down thine altars and killing thy prophets; I am the only one left, and they are after me, to take my life" (1 Kings 19:14, Moffatt).

Most of us know how Elijah must have felt. We can come close to the same panic that is prevalent in this speech to the Eternal the God of hosts. If he is "the only one left," he doesn't feel like sharing this frustration with the world. Especially is this true if he feels he has given the ministry his best shot . . . his best effort . . . his all. Is it any wonder that burnout is the closet sin of the minister? We don't want people feeling sorry for us. It is enough that we feel sorry for ourselves.

One of the first stages of grief is "denial." We refuse to believe that someone has been taken away from us by death. How could this intolerable monster, death, do this to us? Or we refuse to believe that some *thing* precious to us has been taken away from us. We deny it. We bury the hurt. Perhaps that is what burnout is to some ministers. It is a part of the grief process. We have not become all that we think we should have become and therefore we deny the hurt. We face one of the same stages as in grief. If we deny it, we bury it. We keep it in the closet and pretend it does not exist.

MINISTERIAL BURNOUTS ANONYMOUS

Alcoholics have a system. They have a confession. When one of the members speak, the first words are usually, "I am an alcoholic." They feel comfortable in saying it. No one places judgment on them and accuses them of committing the unpardonable sin.

We need a similar system for ministers. The humiliation which is feared when we admit we are near burnout causes us to shy away from the reality and hide in the closet. Perhaps it would be better if we could say with some honest candor, "I am a ministerial burnout." To admit this is the first step in doing something about this predicament. Alcoholics do not go to Alcoholics Anonymous because they want to remain alcoholics. They want to get better. So do ministerial burnouts.

Some of the same reasons an alcoholic would go to an AA meeting could help the minister get his sin out of the closet and go to an MBA (Ministerial Burnouts Anonymous) meeting.

(1) He needs someone to confide in!

He needs to find a group of people who have similar problems, and who are trustworthy. This group of people would be supportive and affirming.

(2) He needs to confess and/or confront the problem!

Ministerial burnout is a real problem. It will not go away with age. It will not go away without a strategy. A group of affirming people can afford him the luxury of being priests to him. A confessional would be neither strange nor humiliating.

(3) He needs to know others care!

Elijah's aloneness was his troublesome factor. He felt no one cared. The minister who faces burnout needs to know that he is cared for by his peers and by friends.

(4) He needs to know that he is OK!

The fact that he is close to burnout does not mean that he is no longer OK as a person. In fact the facing of the problem may be the element of making him stronger.

These four factors, (1) someone to confide in; (2) the need to confess; (3) the need to know others care; and (4) the need to know that he is OK, are reasons why it is difficult for the minister to face ministerial burnout. These are sensitive areas. It is safer to keep these areas of need in the closet. But if he is to affect his own personal growth, he must bring them out of the closet into the real world.

THE TRADE-OFF

Assuming that ministerial burnout (or the potential for burnout) is in the closet, what does the minister gain by bringing it out of the closet and into the open? There must be some kind of trade-off if the risk is to be worth it.

What is to be gained by keeping it in the closet? Louis McBurney, a psychiatrist who pastors ministers, spends most of his energies with ministers and their families. He ministers to their hurts out of his psychiatric training and ministerial calling. He wrote, in regard to this closet theme, "One would expect that here a clergyman (at Marble Retreat in Colorado where he ministers) in pain could surely unburden and feel the support and acceptance of his peers, men who have experienced many of the same hurts. Not so! The masks stay on. . . . Finally, I counsel ministers who have come to Marble Retreat because of emotional problems. Even in this retreat setting with the avowed purpose of getting help they take several hours before they begin to share their feelings. The expectation has been solidly established—clergymen have no hurts; they do not cry or become angry; and for many of them even to show love is difficult."[1] What ministers hope to gain by keeping their human needs in the closet is the distinction of "not being like others." "Not being like others" makes the minister something special. He cannot attain this special appearance, so he feels, if he becomes a human being with the same needs as those to whom he ministers.

The pain, however, of "not being like others" is that there is so much isolation from humanity. The ministers who look for help, even at a place like Marble Retreat, Colorado, continue to hide from each other. He gets "hooked" on isolating himself and feeling this distinction that he would like to believe he is something "special."

McBurney identifies this malady as "emotional self-sufficiency and invulnerability."[2] He goes on to point out the fact that it is folly. In accepting the challenge to be superman, he must leap tall buildings without the capacity to fly. He must dodge bullets without emotionally bulletproof vests. In reality, he is not a superman. He is a man, and a man has manlike feelings of the lack of self-sufficiency and definite feelings of vulnerability.

The trade-off can be described in terms of pride and humility. Pride is that part of the minister that causes him to pretend. He wants others to feel about his worth as he would like to feel but can't quite manage to feel. He cannot manage it himself. He cannot muster enough of the worth out of his own self-esteem, therefore he is prompted to construct self-worth from outside. If he can get others to think he is superman, then maybe it will help his own self-esteem. He may even get to believeing it himself. Some do!

But the pride that causes him to want others to think highly of him has a high cost. It is empty. The payoff is temporary. He begins to want more and more to fill what seems like an almost bottomless pit. He must ask himself a painful question, Is it worth it?

This kind of pride is not only empty, it is *sinful*. We cannot skirt the issue. The closet aspect of hiding our hurts and pains that lead to burn-out is simply *sin*. That, in itself, should be deterrent enough to cause him to face the issue squarely.

Proverbs 11:2 reads, "Pride cometh, then cometh shame." The Greek word, *alazoneia* means "vain boasting or ostentation."[3] It is used in 1 John 2:16, "For all that is in the world, the lust of the flesh, and the lust of the eyes, and the pride of life, is not of the Father, but is of the world."

The opposite of pride is *humility*. Humility is described as *gentleness of spirit*. It is the recognition of one's own lowliness without the help of God. Humility is the prodigal son coming home to the father. Humility is the woman at the well who was conscious of her own sin. Humility is the publican in the presence of the Pharisee. And humility is the minister who is man or woman enough to admit to their own humanity and then be filled with the redeeming quality of love which only comes when one is submitted to the will and presence of God.

The most moving prayer in the New Testament is when Jesus prayed for the "passing" of the cup. He sought another way. He did not cherish the thought of going to the cross. He was both man and God. He was man in that he wished for a less devastating way to establish himself as the Son of God. He was God in that he said, "Nevertheless not my will, but thine, be done." The opposite of pride is humility. But it is not without cost. He must face the pain of the loss of pride.

The trade-off is a release. Others will no longer think of the person who faces burnout and admits it as perfect or infallible. They will release him from his superhumanity. And, like Jesus in Gethsemane, he may not be held in awe by others. He will not be as strong politically. Jesus even suggested that his disciples would deny him. They objected vehemently. But they denied him. Many church members will say, "Go ahead and be human. It is OK for you to admit the fact that you are facing the possibility of burnout." But in their actions, they will be saying, as did the disciples, "How could our minister do this to us. He is supposed to set the model? He is not like us. How dare he be human?" We are released from our expectation to be "not like others," . . . but not without risk!

The trade-off is a *reward*, however, as well as a *re-lease*. The reward is in finding inner strength. Inner strength comes from the practice of humility. Inner strength will reward us by giving us the freedom to get our self-esteem houses off the sand and onto the rock. If we reach back for the resources, we begin to learn *where* to look. Plus, we know it is *there* when we look.

I warned you about my need to build homilies into this pilgrimage. I feel like I just preached a sermon to a group of people who are as adept, or even more so, at building sermonic material as I am. Please give me the privilege of lighting a candle, even if it is for myself, occasionally. After all, what do you expect, searchlights?

OUT OF THE CLOSET AND INTO THE KITCHEN

If we take the private sin of burnout out of the closet, where do we put it? Do we take it outside immediately so that the world may see? Do we tell the world to get it out of our system? That would be unbridled candor. That is no answer. Do we take it to the living room and get comfortable with it? That would be compromise and it would definitely be cowardly because, in a sense, it releases us from the responsibility to discipline ourselves to do something about it.

Do we take it to the bedroom and sleep with it? In other words, will we let it seduce us into thinking it is OK because the rest of the professionals in other vocations are doing it. We create an adulterous relationship with our compromise to burnout because of its enticing quality. The lure of the world of business and industry caused many to see ulcers as a kind of status symbol during the sixties and seventies. Will we allow burnout to be the Jezebel of the eighties?

Many have taken it to the kitchen . . . literally. Recently, a participant in a seminar at the Church Program Training Center discussed a problem he was having in his own vocational direction. He asked for a private consultation. His appearance was best described as obese, not simply overweight. He was heavy. He was forty-eight years old. He had been athletic in his younger years. He was in a church where he felt "stuck." He had been there twelve years. When he went to the church, he was average sized. During the course of his stay, he had gained some one hundred and forty pounds. He described his own problem. With no one placing any deliberate judgment on him, he began to unfold his story. After he had been there five years, he began to feel that his every move was under scrutiny. He had been the recipient of much undeserved criticism (at least, in his opinion). Two staff members had resigned with considerable conflict between the two of them and him.

He said he began to feel "empty" almost all of his waking moments. He felt no support from others. He was not being refueled by the affirmation of his church members. He felt the emptiness so dramatically that he began to eat to try to fill it. He was "starved" and was hungry for the kind of food he could not get. Anything edible was in jeopardy if within his reach. Fortunately, while attending the seminar on Church Staff Relations, he had come to a reawakening. Quite honestly he had been reawakened before. He came to the seminar because of the reawakening. He decided to recommit his own life to his personal mission. He had decided to begin a diet planned for him by his physician. The best part of his decision was that he had decided that he had something about himself to be proud of. He had regained some of his self-esteem. He said he was going to seek out some friends who had helped him in years past. He was going to fill his needs in other ways than killing himself by eating.

THE BENDS SYNDROME

Don't come out of the closet too fast. When deep-sea divers come up too fast, they get the bends. They have excruciating pain. The oxygen balance in the body is in shock. It is not only painful, it is dangerous.

If ministers of the inclination to hide their burnout are to face it realistically, they must avoid the bends syndrome. They should not try to come up too quickly.

Let me explain. A minister attended a group experience where openness was the accepted modus operandi. He looked at himself in ways that his forty-one years in ministry had not permitted him before. He was elated. He was excited. He could not wait to get back home and tell someone. He told his wife what had happened to him. He had discovered the reason why he had had difficulty relating to one of the most influential people in his church. He had cut off communications with this person some five years before. This person, he discovered, was the reincarnation of his own father. The feelings he conjured up were that of a child being disciplined when the member had criticized his compulsive behavior in dealing with other staff members.

He called the member and arranged a time for them to get together. He "unloaded" on the member. He not only called attention to his own actions but called attention to the actions of the church member as well.

The shock was too much for the church member. He accepted the explanation, even though he did not fully understand. But soon thereafter, he left the church and took several other close and intimate followers with him. The minister had the bends. He was coming up too soon.

Later, the minister had occasion to check out the reasons for the member leaving through another trusted friend of both persons involved. The member who left the church complained of the pastor's "emotional instability." "He used that conference as an excuse to attack me!" was the statement quoted to the minister from another member.

Rather than "getting everything straightened out immediately" as was his desire, he had created another problem altogether. He had confused the member with his "apparently unpredictable" behavior. Our perception is different from others. We must give them room to be who they are. Otherwise we get the bends from their shock. Both get hurt!

The member could not help the fact that he reminded the pastor of his father. That was unfortunate but it could happen to anyone. Rather than confront the member with this liberating truth, he could have approached the situation more slowly. He could have allowed his body to adjust to the oxygen level with more time and patience. In his excitement from the redemptive revelation to himself he was looking for the surface quickly. I am in danger of mixing metaphors but let me take one more step. Bear with me. He almost drowned the member who was on the surface. He reached up for the safety of an explanation but he drug the member under the emotional waters because the member was not able to swim with the onslaught of the pastor's emotional garbage which had been redeemed.

The bottom line of this questionable metaphor is that a minister must be careful in how he handles the sin of burnout. It is essential that it be brought out of the closet. It is even more essential that it be brought out with care and consideration. Do not announce the coming out too loudly. Take it slowly. Allow the body to adjust to the dramatic changes.

PACK YOUR BAG BEFORE COMING OUT OF THE CLOSET

Some equipment is necessary when the minister brings the problem of burnout out of the closet.

(1) First, pack some *tenacity*.

Look inside yourself and pack some toughness to get through the painful ordeal. Then determine to stick until you have thoroughly faced the problem. This may be the toughest part of the journey. Dag Hammarskjold wrote,

> The longest journey
> Is the journey inwards.
> Of him who has chosen his destiny,
> Who has started upon his quest
> For the source of his being
> (Is there a source?).
> He is still with you,
> But without relation,
> Isolated in your feeling
> Like one condemned to death
> Or one whom imminent farewell
> Prematurely dedicates
> To the loneliness which is the final lot of all.[4]

Be tenacious about the journey inward before you announce that you have begun your journey out of burnout.

(2) Pack some *energy*.

You cannot get younger. That is certain. But you can find some energy cells and maximize them. You can find your energy peaks and use them. Finding energy areas in the lives of ministers may be one of the biggest challenges. But it can be done. Find some new uses for aggression. Study the whole concept of aggression and determine to turn this energy making arena into assertiveness which is the direct result of channeled energy.

Leroy "Satchel" Paige, a professional baseball player, who once played with the Cleveland Indians, coined six injunctions for staying young. These might help in channeling the energy necessary for breaking out of the closet.

> Avoid fried meats which angry up the blood.
> If your stomach disputes you, lie down and pacify it with cool thoughts.
> Keep the juices flowing by jangling around gently as you move.
> Go very lightly on the vices, such as carrying on in society.
> The society ramble ain't restful.
> Avoid running at all times.
> Don't look back. Something might be gainin' on you.[5]

These helpful hints from Satchel Paige might be helpful if your imagination is active. They were helpful to me.

Dr. Joseph Ungar, an internal medicine specialist, wrote in a medical journal that Satchel Paige's "Rules for Long Life"[6] were the forerunner of the current brand of preventive medicine which many doctors are prescribing for patients in the 1980s. Indeed, it is the heart of *wholistic medicine* which is a revolutionary idea in good physical and emotional health.

(3) Pack some *innoculation*.

It is essential that the minister be innoculated to the inordinate pressures on his own person and on his life with his family. The minister can do much to innoculate himself. He can be careful in the way that he begins his self-disclosure. He can take care in the way he reaches out to others when he hears them in their need. He will need this innoculation. It will be vital to his preparation to face his bold new world.

Robert Raines wrote, "There is a lot of pressure in society today to be a warm, intimate, self-revelatory person. It is good, of course, to be more personally available to each other, and I am one of those who in recent years has been grateful to be broken up and made more human, more vulnerable, more real. At the same time, the Kingdom of God is not to be identified with a constant encounter group. There continues to be value in privacy, in discretion, and in the appropriateness of the time and place and persons involved in self-revelation."[7] In other words, as the minister comes out of the closet to reveal his vacuum of burnout, he must be discretionary about the way he reveals it. He cannot afford full-time navel gazing. It is too expensive in terms of energy. He can be innoculated against a lot of unnecessary pain if he does so with discrimination.

(4) Pack some *future focus*.

It would be easy to regress. Going back to the good old days is a very special game for older persons. It can be a chosen game for the minister. He remembers in his youthful days when he could make things happen. It would be so easy to conjure up some reasons why he could make things happen then and cannot seem to do so today. But there is a hook in this regression. It preoccupies the mind and energy so much that it is difficult or impossible to focus on the future. Focusing on the future is a good piece of equipment for the minister who is about to come out of the closet with his sin of burnout. The temptation will be to focus on the past. Far less energy is expended in focusing on the past than on the future.

One minister wrote in his *Reflections paper* in one of our Personal and Professional Growth Courses (conducted at the Church Program Training Center, Nashville, Tennessee) that, his mind still conjured up all kinds of creative activity, but that his body did not cooperate. "I still have the same fantastic ideas I did when I was twenty-five, but the energy level is not as high. I want to perform, but my body won't let me. I keep asking myself, What was it that gave me such an incentive to act that I have not been able to do during the past five years since I reached fifty?"

What are the benefits of focusing on the future?! Barbara Fried wrote a book on *The Middle Age Crisis*. One passage was particularly relevant. "As long as the middlescent concentrates on what used to be—that is, on the disagreeable fact that strength, sexual vigor, activity, youthful beauty, stamina, and potential are waning—he (or she) will never be able to accept the idea that experience, assurance, substance, skill, achievement, wisdom, success, (and) the judgment to see what is truly important more than compensate for the disappearance of youthful power."[8]

Please give me permission to belabor this point a bit. Suppose you pack your bag. You have what you think is necessary for making the trip. But for the first two or three days, you keep asking yourself if you packed appropriately. Maybe I should have taken the other suit which I left in my closet. Never having gone to Alaska before, when I went, I was anxious about taking the right and appropriate clothes. Sure enough I did not take the right clothes. However, it gave me an excuse to buy some of the things that I really wanted. Although I could not afford all that I felt was necessary, I found some compensation in buying what I could afford. I now have one set of insulated underwear which came directly from Alaska. It was one of those surprises which makes a trip like that interesting. You cannot know if you have packed everything you will be using when you come out of the closet. It will be risky. You will need some additional clothes. But if you focus on the future you will already be ahead of the game.

In summary, if you pack your bag before you come out of the closet, you will have:

(1) packed some tenacity;
(2) packed some energy;
(3) packed some innoculation;
(4) and packed some future focus.

DEALING WITH THE SAMSON CONNECTION

Before moving on to burnout in the minister's home, could we deal with one more element in the closet sin of the minister? What about the Samson connection?

You remember Samson! He was that Old Testament hero who had all kinds of strength for all kinds of tasks. He was a favorite subject of our Bible study as children. His remains one of the beautiful stories which bears telling again and again.

There is one particular aspect of Samson which catches the fancy of almost every minister. After he "did his thing" with the jawbone of a donkey, he remarked "With a donkey's jawbone I have made donkeys of them. With a donkey's jawbone I have killed a thousand men" (Judg. 15:16, NIV). It seems a lot more fun to make donkeys out of the church members who give us the most trouble than it does to adjust to the fact that if we cut away our assumed strength, they might have the upper hand. Most all of us have a need to be a bit of a hero. We would rather be the one causing stress than be the recipient of stress. It is more fun to be the carrier of stress than the stressee.

Then along came Delilah. Every Samson has a Delilah. It may not be in the form of a woman, but something or someone will find our Achilles' heels, our weak spot, and expose it. She exploited his weakness. She did not discover it easily. She stayed with it though until she had worn him down.

A great deal has been said and written in the past two or three years about how the minister can best establish a "power base." Establishing power has been a popular theme even at a denominational level. Many feel that the controversy over right and left wing theology is more about power than about biblical accuracy. It is only natural that the minister would wish to establish his own power within the confines of his church Samson had the power. He was gifted with great strength. He was also gifted with gamesmanship. He was constantly hassling. First, he hassled with his wife over a riddle. Then he hassled with Delilah about the origin of his strength. Most people who have a way with power have a gift (or a curse) with hassling. Usually the powerful people come up on the winning side of the ledger. But it is just as certain that most of these powerful persons meet their Waterloo. Samson met his with Delilah. She outwitted him.

The lesson to be learned in the Samson connection has to do with coming out of the closet without deliberately drawing out the Delilahs. It was apparent that Samson liked to play "one-upmanship." He needed someone with whom to play the game. He placed others in a win-lose predicament. Samson wanted to make donkeys of his adversaries. He paraded his strength. It is certain that there is strength in facing the problem of burnout. But it is just as certain that we do not need to prove to the world that we can do it. It we do, we can be certain that there will be a Delilah or two waiting to groom our behavior.

A SHATTERED DREAM

Perhaps the strongest reason that burnout is so difficult to face is because it is somehow symbolic of the shattered dream. No one wants to give up on his dream. The minister has a sense of calling. He has developed this sense of calling into and through a dream. He may not have the dream in focus as much as he likes but he has a rather vivid idea of the reality nevertheless.

He pretends. If he buries his sense of hopelessness, no one will know . . . not even himself. He hides the potential burnout because the dream was so important to him. He is too idealistic, in most cases, to structure his dream into a particular church, or a particular ministry, but he has an idea or glimpse of something he would like to accomplish . . . or someone he would like to be like. He considers the likes of Billy Graham, or John Claypool, or W. A. Criswell, or John Bisagno, or Al McEachern, and he chooses one that is most like him. In his dream he wants a name similar to those who already have prominent names. But he has not reached the pinnacle of "nameness" as quickly as he thought he could or should. The dream begins to become distorted. He has begun to feel burnout before he has arrived. Is it strange that he wants to hide the closet sin of burnout from those peers who are significant to him? Of course not! He is not strange . . . he is human.

2

Burnout in the Minister's Home

He that loveth his own wife loveth himself: for no man ever hated his own flesh; but nourisheth and cherisheth it, even as Christ also the church (Eph. 5:28b-29, ASV).

One minister's wife complained, "I have never been so angry! If it had been another woman, I at least would have known how to fight it. Like this, I am helpless. He has deprived me of the affection and intimacy I deserve. He neglects me even when he is in the house. I can't take much more." She may be the exception but she deserves to be heard. It will be useful as a warning . . . even to the most compatible.

The minister's home suffers first. It is the wife and children who begin to see the minister in his listless and "don't care" attitude which precedes or includes burnout. It is the wife who must struggle to pick him up when he comes home from a day with troubled persons and troublesome deacons. The children have very little understanding about the unusual and harsh discipline which they occasionally receive as the result of a frustrating day.

One wife of a minister said the truth was brought home to her in dramatic reality when her five-year-old son grumbled, "Dad is no fun, anymore. All he does when he comes home is sit in front of the television."

The fault, however, does not lie fully in the lap of the minister. His wife and family contribute. His wife and family may be a *major* contributory factor. She may be just as burned out as he The children may be just as burned out as they. Our objective is *not to place fault* though. Our objective is to try to find out how to know when we are near burnout and then what to do about it. This includes the family of the minister.

In defense of the minister who was being accused in the opening paragraph of this chapter, the wife had a history of unfulfilled dreams and unsatisfied needs. She had spent most of the twenty-two years of their marriage complaining about being a minister's wife, and living in a fish bowl, and suddenly she finds herself the recipient of a mate who had some complaints of his own. He just did not feel like he could face the same neurotic church members day after day for the rest of his life . . . especially since he was getting virtually no help from home.

WHY MINISTERS' WIVES CANNOT GIVE REFUGE IN BURNOUT

It is impossible for the wife to bail the minister out when he faces burnout. She has neither the equipment nor the want to, in most cases. Neither should she be expected to do so.

(I am aware that there are scores and scores of ministers who are women. In that case, the discussion under this topic should have been labeled *spouses*. There is one major flaw in this reasoning. The premise behind this book is that burnout is a syndrome among male ministers. There are obviously many women who are facing some of the same problems in burnout, but the experience of this author has been almost totally limited to men. I write about those things with which I am familiar. Burnout affects women, but most of the women who are affected are the wives of those ministers who are confronting this very difficult problem.)

Lucille Lavender is a minister's wife. She speaks from the experience of one who has "been there." Listen as she describes the expectations of the ministers' wives. Perhaps we can learn why the minister's wife should not be expected to give an inordinate amount of help to the minister facing burnout.

A minister's wife should be attractive, but not too much so; have nice clothes, but not too nice (she will always be applauded for making her clothes); have a nice basic hair-do, but not too nice; be friendly, but not too friendly; be aggressive and greet everyone, especially visitors, but not too aggressive; intelligent, but not too intelligent; educated, but not too educated; down-to-earth, but not too much so; capable, but not too capable; charming but not too charming; and be herself—but not openly.[1]

When I first read that passage, I said, "Wow! I wish I had said that!" For all those ministers' wives who have lived under these unrealistic expectations . . . especially for twenty-two years . . . I not only applaud them, I reiterate the fact that they should not be expected to bail him out. She cannot. She has spent too much energy making things right herself. She has no magic wand to wave and make things OK with her struggling husband.

A wife of a minister has a special set of criteria to meet. Some of these she established for herself. Some, others establish for her. In a ministers' wives survey, some of these feelings are revealing:

"I miss being able to have special friends that we can just enjoy ourselves with, without feeling we are leaving others out." Another wrote, "We are programmed women. Programmed to behave like, act like, say yes to, whatever the church—especially the women—want us to do, according to their whims or personal preferences." Still another wrote, "To tell you the truth, I don't fit in. I prefer to be alone. I'm very much an introvert and I feel I've made a complete flop as a minister's wife. But my husband insists he likes me the way I am, and that he didn't marry me to be his assistant. His attitude is all that makes life worthwhile."[2]

To every rule there is an exception. There will be many wives who will give the necessary help to their husbands. These wives are exceptional. Most, in my judgment, could use some support themselves. In fact, most wives of ministers who are in burnout will be going through some form of burnout themselves.

Let me be more specific. Some reasons can be sorted out. These reasons can explain why many ministers' wives cannot give all the help necessary.

(1) They feel isolated themselves.

Many wives of ministers are spending so much time feeling that they are isolated from humanity that it will be virtually impossible for them to know where to get plentiful doses of assistance for their husbands.

Of course, this does not mean that she is isolated from the humanity of "activities." Most are active to the point of dizziness. She attends women's meetings. She is invited to religious luncheons. She is official greeter on Sunday and talks to the visitors. She may even get to sit at the head table at important community banquets. But she is still isolated. She may be active to the point of frenzy and still feel that she is soundly isolated from the intimacy which is necessary for her to be fulfilled in her role as a distinctive person.

Again, not all ministers' wives feel this isolation. Many, perhaps most, are gregarious and get a certain satisfaction from the social activities which are surrounding the minister's home. Then again, not all ministers will face burnout in the same way. Some ministers may be fortunate enough not to need what other ministers need. We may argue the case, however. Many of the ones who have convinced themselves that they can meet their husband's needs as he goes through burnout sublimate much satisfaction for themselves. Many ministers' wives deny that they are facing isolation themselves and live with the masks that many church members expect them to wear, but not without some sacrifice.

(2) They feel they must compete for their husband's time.

Ministers' wives want their husbands to meet their needs on occasion. If the minister goes home every day to get his own needs met, eventually the well will run dry. One young wife of a thirty-one-year minister explained, "I cannot give the replenished energy necessary for my husband. In fact, when he comes home it's his time to assume some responsibility. I feel he should have the privilege of changing diapers, watching the streets, and yelling at the kids. I need him. I can't pump life into three kids for ten hours and an exhausted husband for the rest of the evening. He's got to find the extra energy right along with me."

A certain amount of anger is natural. She only sees the tired soul who crawls in the door. She does not see that he has spent four hours visiting hospitals, two hours visiting disgruntled deacons, and two and one-half hours preparing for the Wednesday evening services. She does not know of the phone call that started his day when Mrs. Alexander reprimanded him sharply for visiting Mrs. Grey when she was in the hospital and failed to visit her sister who was in the hospital in the next city (thirty-six miles away). She simply remembers that two of the children were quarreling when she got them off to school. She took the baby to the doctor and found that he wanted payment on the spot because the last bill had not been paid. She was the one who felt the embarrassment when one of the members overheard the nurse ask for an immediate payment. She gave the nurse a check but had grave doubts about whether there was money in the bank to cover it. It is no small wonder that she feels some anger when he complains about what a bad day he had. She is not so sympathetic when he uses the new word he heard at the seminar last week, *burnout*, and how he might be facing this difficult problem. He will have some difficulty in getting all the needed support from his wife.

(3) They feel they must match up.

The thought may never occur to the wives who have it all together. It may even sound spiritually lacking. But there are those wives who feel that they are expected (by their husbands, no less) to match up with the wives of young and no-so-young executives who seem to have unlimited resources to look their best in the latest fashions. The budget the minister and his family live on is woefully lacking when compared to these other professionals. Yet they are human. They have personal needs and wants. They want to look their best. But they must look their best on less than adequate resources.

(4) They feel they have no privacy.

At this point, I was struggling. I wanted to be fair to both the minister and his wife. Although I feel strongly that the minister must not have unrealistic expectations of his wife when he faces possible burnout, I was not certain whether I was seeing the problem from the point of view of the wife. So I asked my wife. She was the wife of a pastor for twelve years. She also feels a liberation in expressing her feelings about the abuse of the wife of the minister . . . especially by the congregation. She had no hesitance in her first reply, "Everybody knows your business!"

I replied, "You mean you did not feel we had any privacy?"

"That, too!" she said. I got the meesage.

That problem takes its toll. It drains the energy of a wife who needs privacy. Plus . . . there are added measures to make sure that everyone does *not* know all your business. That takes energy, too! The pains we took in being secretive about where we got the new television set were deliberate. The games played when being questioned about where we ate dinner the night before were uncomfortable. Once we took a weekend trip (Friday and Saturday . . . not Sunday) with a couple who were marginal in their attendance and commitment to the church. It was late Saturday night when we got back home. Sure enough we had a phone call at 10:15 PM.

"I hate to bother you at this late hour."

"That's OK, Mrs. Mattingly, we were just getting home anyway," my wife responded. Mrs. Mattingly knew that, since she lived only a quarter of a mile from the parsonage.

"I just wanted you to know that my grandson checked by the parsonage several times this weekend to make sure everything was OK."

"Thank you, Mrs. Mattingly."

"I hope you had a good trip, wherever it was you went," she hinted.

"We had a much-needed time to get away, and we certainly did enjoy it," said my wife.

"Well, I hope you did some things to get your mind off all the problems of the church. I know how much your husband has been worrying about the Weaver family."

"I don't think he thought about anything but the ball game," at which time my wife knew she had been hooked.

"Oh, is that where you went? to the ball game?"

It is true, everybody knows your business . . . or would like to. I have yet to fully understand the morbid curiosity of church members about the whereabouts of their ministers.

(5) They feel there is a certain discrimination.

Many wives of ministers feel the boundaries are pretty well defined. She may have permission to attend some functions. If the function is of such a nature as to be devoid of pure joy and celebration, then she certainly may come. But if the occasion is one where there will be a particularly interesting speaker, or celebrity, then it is doubtful that she will be invited. Lavender elaborates, Some of the reasons why she is not invited to participate in these special or regular functions are:

1. We didn't think to ask her.
2. She is different.
3. She is too busy.
4. She would not be interested.
5. She would not fit in.
6. She does not have the social needs other women do.
7. She is not qualified.[3]

The bottom line, in regard to discrimination, is that many wives feel that they are treated "differently." They are not like other women. They should not act like other women, they feel. They do not think like other women. Consequently, how could they be expected to enjoy the same things other women enjoy? It would be comforting if some ministers could empathize with their wives to the extent of understanding these feelings of discrimination. Whether she is actually discriminated against is beside the point. If she "feels" she is discriminated against, she will have little to give when he feels burned out unless he can first (or at least at the same time) give her the understanding and affirmation she needs.

DON'T RUB EVEN IF IT HURTS

It may be acceptable on the basketball floor. If the elbow of an opposing player catches your rib, then, by all means, do not display hurt by rubbing the rib. This would mean giving in. This would mean accepting the fact that the opponent is capable of getting to you. You can't have the opponent think that you are so human that you hurt. You would then be at a disadvantage.

But where does it say this should spill over into a marriage? Especially the marriage of a minister? What does it say to the spouse when you rub where it hurts? It says "Hey, I'm in pain, and I need some sympathy!" The freedom to admit that we are in pain is healing in itself. The denial or distortion of pain contributes to more pain. One reason why burnout has become a reality is that the partners in the family of the minister do not feel free to rub where it hurts.

What we are really describing is *intimacy*. Intimacy is the revelation of our humanity to another and believing they care anyway. Howard and Charlotte Clinebell wrote a classic book on intimacy, *The Intimate Marriage*. In the description of "Barriers to Intimacy," they describe what these barriers are. These are especially helpful to us who are searching for the strategies to relieve some of the pressure building.

We cannot seem to get a proper perspective of the sense of identity. If we cannot know ourselves, then it follows that it will be difficult to know our spouse. One barrier is "emotional immaturity."[4] A person is most likely emotionally immature if they have a primary commitment to their parents rather than to each other. If each is more concerned with his own needs than the other's needs then, this, too, indicates emotional immaturity.

Another barrier is the "fear of being hurt."[5] The most common way their barrier has of uncovering its head is through massive appreciation. One partner would not be caught dead criticizing the other. The entire relationship is built on accolades and flowers, candy and love letters. All the minister has ever heard is what a remarkable husband he is, and how wonderful his attention for the family is, and then when he hurts so badly, he does not feel free to express his pain because it would destroy the myth. So he holds it in. He denies the hurt, and the slow burn continues. He just cannot bring himself to let his wife and family down. One day a youthful forty-eight-year-old minister of this nature just did not come home. He was not heard from for twelve days. The wife and family thought he had been kidnapped, or worse. He finally did show up 2,000 miles away, in a motel, broke, and barely remembering who he was or what had happened during the twelve-day ordeal. After sorting his life out and getting the pieces put back together, one of the most marvelous learning experiences that resulted from the painful experience was, in his words, "The fact that I could turn to my wife and family and find support." He explained that he simply did not feel that it was possible up until this time. He was surprised that they cared for him even when he was hurting.

The Clinebells share still another barrier to intimacy: "low self-esteem and guilt feelings."[6] It is mandatory that the minister learn to cope. He should not tolerate low self-esteem. If he pictures himself as of little value, then feelings of being unlovable are inevitable. It sounds strange for a minister to be dealing with the problems of low self-esteem. He is the person who is trying to help others build their own self-esteem. He is trying to teach the magnificent creative power of God and the worth of the individual as a result of this creative power.

But how can one spot a minister with low self-esteem and guilt feelings? Some symptoms are evident.

One, he uses the phrase frequently, "I did nothing. Just give the credit to the Lord." At first thought, that sounds like a beautiful and humble statement to hear. On second thought, he may be rejecting a support statement. He may feel it was not really meant for him. "I am not worth that compliment," is a way of being falsely modest or a way of rejecting the affection of another person. Usually, when a compliment is paid, the person is trying to say, I care about you. You are worth something to me. If he rejects the compliment, the minister may be saying, I refuse to believe that you care. I refuse to believe that I am worth something. Therefore, be honest.

Two, he may be just the opposite. He may respond to a compliment with, "Yeah, I know! I'm great, aren't I?" At that point, the person who has given the compliment is supposed to laugh. He has rejected the compliment. What he has really said is, "Don't be serious with me, I am not worth it." It is uncomfortable to think that I may really be worth something, and that I have something to give. Therefore I reject it with statements of false pride. That helps release the tension of the compliment. It keeps me from having to deal with the compliment. . . . Don't rub even if it does hurt! Also, don't rub even if it feels good! Someone may think you like it and you just can't have the image blown.

A third symptom is seen in the man who says, "I just cannot acknowledge affirmation because if they get past my shell they may see what a phony I really am." Of course, he does not say this aloud. He is much more discreet with whom he trusts this honesty. Their guilt causes them to remain in what some have termed *alien territory*.[7] Somehow those who share this third symptom fear vulnerability. They must not get close to people. Some ministers even rationalize that it is biblical. You just cannot get close to people, they will say. . . . because people will take advantage of you when you least expect it.

It may be healing to be vulnerable. It may also be risky. In my judgment, it is worth the gamble.

CHILDREN ARE AFFECTED, TOO

Burnout may occur when the minister's children are small. Frequently, the symptoms of burnout occur when children are in their developmental years. They are somewhere between the ages of seven and eighteen. Obviously, there are many exceptions. Children are affected by the changes which occur in their parents. Especially is this true with the professional person. The minister and his family are a part of the professional community.

No one else faces the same set of circumstances in growing up as does a PK (Preacher's Kid). These persons do not choose to grow up in a glass house. They have no choice at all. They have expectations thrust on them. They cannot live up to all the expectations. They may not want to live up to them. If so, then the rebelliousness of the PK's may be an additional problem for both the children and the parents. Burnout may be made much more complex when the children present a specialized set of problems which have been the result of the glass-house syndrome.

Undeniably, there is some status. Some PK's are able to cope with the situation because of the recognition afforded them. Some seem to thrive on this recognition. Although it may not be received without some resentment, there seems to be some preference for the PK's under some situations. On the other hand, many PK's deeply resent the particularization of them. "I don't want to be treated differently," said one. "I want to be treated like one of the gang."

Another PK's response was: "Everything I do is magnified one hundred times. I can't skip prayer meeting without someone calling attention to it."

And when one does get into trouble, it reflects on the entire family. A lot of emphasis is placed on the scriptural reference, "One that ruleth well his own house, having his children in subjection with all gravity; (For if a man know not how to rule his own house, how shall he take care of the church of God?)" (1 Tim. 3:4-5). A minister must feel this weight. At times it must feel like an albatross. When one seventeen-year-old boy (a PK) was arrested for possession of marijuana, the whole city seemed to know. His father felt paranoid. He felt he could not walk down the street without someone pointing to him. Fortunately, the church stuck by him. The church supported him through a very difficult time and he survived the ordeal. In fact, he is still at the same church.

LOVE IN THE HOME IS SPELLED T-I-M-E

It is difficult to measure the average time a minister spends with his family in comparison to other professional or community-minded men. Perhaps the minister would be far out of line in this comparison. In conversations and counseling with persons in other professions, it appears the time factor is very similar. However, the problem is still a very real and identifiable one: that is, children of professional persons need the *time* of the parents if they are to build a structure.

The family is the oldest institution. The family is the way the minister and his wife lead by example. The family must give them ways to meet their own needs and at the same time, meet the needs of the children in the home.

John Wynn, in his book, *Pastoral Ministry to Families*, "states that if a minister devotes all his time and his energy to making a success of his profession, life in the manse (parsonage, to Baptists) must suffer. It is possible for him to gain a church and lose a home. The fitness of a pastor to assume the cure of souls is roughly proportionate to his quality as a husband and father. . . . His sense of values needs constant, prayerful review lest he subjugate family welfare to *administrivia* under the mistaken assumption that these comprise the Kingdom of God."[8]

The Disciples of Christ denomination formulated for their clergy a code which we would all do well to heed: "I will be fair to my family and will endeavor to give them the *time* and consideration to which they are entitled."[9]

A number of studies and research findings suggest that the minister spends about twenty-five hours a week at home regardless of the size of his church membership or the number of his offspring still at home. (It is interesting, however, that a minister with four or more children spent only nineteen hours at home. If my mathematics is correct, that is about six hours less than the average. I wonder if that is being fair to the poor wife who has very little choice in staying home.)[10]

Many ministers feel guilty taking the time to be with their families especially at the expense of forsaking some activity at the church. It should be the other way around. He should feel guilty if he spends too much time at the church at the expense of his family. He is sensitive to meeting the needs of his church. That is his professional responsibility. However, he is also responsible to his family. He must be reminded of that responsibility.

It is not so much the amount of time spent at home. It is the unpredictability of the time spent at home. The children of ministers at a conference at Ridgecrest Baptist Assembly in the summer of 1978 discussed with animation the frustration about the unpredictability of the time their fathers were home. Even when he was at home the phone was constantly ringing, they felt. His energy and attention was more on the phone than on them.

I spent a few days in the home of a pastor friend of mine while leading a conference in his church. On the day he was supposed to have set aside for his "day off" he and I lounged around the house. Things went pretty slowly during the day. There were a few phone calls from church members, but not an inordinate amount. When 5:00 rolled around it was a different story. By this time his teenage son and teenage daughter were home from school. The church members were also home from their work. The phone began to ring. The pastor was on the phone constantly from 5:00 until 7:00, at which time we were supposed to eat. While he talked on the phone, I talked with his son as the two of us watched television. I asked if the calls were unusual. He laughed. "This is a slow day," he mused. "I am used to it, though. We know that we can't get a word in edgewise to Dad while he is here. And besides, when he is not here, he is at church with them. They see a lot more of him than we do." He laughed again, but he was not amused. It was a laugh of exasperation.

"How do you feel about the fact that it is hard to get the privilege of talking with your dad?" I asked.

"Oh, I'm used to it. I don't have to like it though. I sometimes feel selfish about wanting to talk to him more."

CAPITALIZE ON TOGETHERNESS

I kept asking myself, Where did we go wrong? What can we do about this atrocious situation that makes us forsake our own family while we try to teach other families how to capitalize on their togetherness?

I have a few practical suggestions how we might help our ministers find the necessary togetherness with their families.

(1) First, get the story over to him while he is being trained to minister to the needs of members of his own flock. Teach courses in college and seminary that create more redemptive and guiding guilt on him to tend to the needs of his own family first. This could solve more than one problem. It would help the minister to deal with the potential problem of divorce which often appears when the minister is acutely negligent. This is especially true if the cause of the divorce in the minister's family is because he has not given his spouse and family enough of his time.

(2) Second, we need conferences, workshops, and seminars in every state and all over the world for our missionaries to help wives and children of the minister confront the problem head on. In other words, they should not feel selfish, as the young son did, because they want to be with their dad. It is their right. That takes some hard training. We made a beginning at our conference centers for two or three years in the late '70s. We had special conferences for PK's. We also have more frequent conferences for wives at these conference centers. State conventions must spend more of their energies trying to provide ways for the wives and children of ministers to learn how to capitalize on the time of their husbands and fathers.

(3) We need more communication through our established state papers and denominational publications to help both the minister and his family to block out time for each other. Our state paper editors could spend more of their readable and influential editorials on helping the minister and his family to release the guilt of wanting to spend time with each other.

(4) We need training programs for lay persons. We need to help church members understand how important it is for the minister and his family to spend time together. They can help him relieve his guilt-motivated actions of wanting to be the bride at every wedding and the corpse at every funeral. An encouraging and supportive word from an influential layman can work miracles in the mind-set of the minister. We must help those influential laymen in two ways. We must, first, help the laymen or laywomen know how influential they are. Then we must help them know how to speak the words to relieve the guilt. We must encourage them not to heap accolades on the "busyness" of their minister if he is neglecting his family.

I have two children. During their early life they were the children of a pastor. During the past few years they have been the children of a minister who works for a denomination. I think they both see me as a committed Christian and a dedicated minister. They know I like my work. They understand, at least, to some degree, what my calling into the ministry means to me. They are very different. One of the children enjoys the inside of the workings of the church. The other is more complicated. I have spent a lot of time trying to understand the difference. One of my children will read this book. The other will read it only if he is marooned on an island with nothing left to do but read one book that is his only source of recreation.

Many times I have asked myself the question that most normal parents have asked themselves at one time or another: "If I had my life to live over again with my family what would I do differently?" I just do not know the answer to that question. Maybe "time" is the answer. Maybe it would be easier to understand the complexity of my children if I had spent more time with them. I have spent a great deal of time feeling the "urge" to be at a church committee meeting when I have been at home with them. On the other hand, I have spent a great deal of time feeling the "urge" to be with them when I was at a church committee meeting. As I write this, I ponder the thought that maybe the complexity of my children is not nearly so much with them as it is with me. How could I possibly want to be two places at one time? Am I the only minister-father who has ever felt that strange "urge"?

IF I HAD IT TO LIVE OVER AGAIN

It is very difficult to conclude this chapter on the minister's family. Burnout certainly affects the minister's family. I want to conclude by continuing this question I pondered above, "If I had my life to live over again with my family what would I do differently?"

. . ."*I would not treat my wife as an assistant pastor.*" But more than that, I would do everything within my power to keep the church members from treating her as an assistant pastor. No wonder she had no privacy. Those who *could not* reach the pastor *could* reach the pastor's wife at home. She is a good substitute if the pastor cannot be reached, some neurotic church members reason. Some church members will always view the minister's wife as an assistant pastor.

. . ."*I would not permit my children to be seen as little ministers.*" In spite of all my efforts, some church members still saw my son and daughter as little ministers. They were sorely disappointed if their behavior did not live up to their expectations. They have rights, too! My children have the right to be free to make the same mistakes you and I did. I would spend more time helping them know that they were not little ministers. I would help church members understand it, too.

. . . "*I would spend more time helping my wife have more privacy.*" Your wife may not need it. My wife did. And, I am ashamed to say, I didn't do nearly enough to help her to have the privacy she needed so badly.

. . . "*I would spend more time helping both my wife and children find a sense of meaning in their own lives.*" I did not contribute nearly enough in this area. I could have done so much more. In many ways, my wife is more professional than I. I did very little to help her fulfill enough of her professional desires. I spent a great deal of time with the attitude that my vocation was the highest priority in life. God calls us into ministry. That makes it a high priority, but it should not be at the expense of the family of the minister. They have a right to a sense of meaning, too.

I would spend more time fishing with my son. He does not enjoy golf as I do. I was selfish. He deserved to have his needs met recreationally as well as I.

. . ."*I would do more to help my wife not feel trapped.*" I am not exactly sure how I would do this. But she was not comfortable feeling obligated to attend as many functions as she attended. She was not excited about going to as many circle meetings as she attended. I would try to relieve some of the guilt I heaped on her.

. . . "*I would start earlier in encouraging the church to permit me to buy my own home.*" There is very little security in living in the church parsonage. Some choose to do so. More power to them. I want to feel the comfort of knowing I have an investment in my own home. My wife and family do, too. Most churches are wise enough to negotiate those needs with pastors nowadays. It has not always been so. In fact, many churches still need training in this area. There is a peculiar sense in which the wife and family feel "owned" by living in a church-owned parsonage. It is always "their" rooms when painting time or redecorating time comes around. My wife and family enjoy the sense of ownership of our home.

. . . "*I would do more to help my wife and family feel comfortable in having close friends.*" Without exception, in every church where I was pastor, we negotiated this issue. We always found some families we wanted to get closer to. Sometimes we did. Of course, we had to pay the price. There was jealousy. It was worth it. I would do it even more today were I pastoring. The risks are worth the dividends. Close friends are a necessity, especially to the family.

I have never understood the rationale I have heard so frequently— "You just can't get close to people." I just do not believe that belief is justified in my life.

. . . "*I would get the help of my family in handling criticism.*" I was more the martyr type. I thought I could handle it myself. I should have relied on them more. They deserve the opportunity to share the misery. They could help. They could give me more objectivity. Sometimes my wife would have liked very much to handle the criticism herself. Once she did. She did an excellent job. She was much more direct than I. She got right to the point, got her part said. The issue was settled in her mind. She did not spend sleepless nights worrying if she made someone so mad that they might quit the church. I probably would have done so. In fact, I have a few times. On the other hand, there were a few times that I was overjoyed that I was able to settle a dispute without her. Had she been involved, wow!

Those are a few of the things I could have done better with my family. It would have helped. There are many things I did right. I am proud of those. I loved them. I cared for them. Their needs were met. We solved our problems for the most part. We worked through some bad times but we lived through some wonderful times. My family was, and is, a part of my life and ministry. They are a part of the burnout or the lack of burnout in every minister's life.

3

Burnout in the Minister's Professional Life

There are people who go on indefinitely preparing for life instead of living it.—*Paul Tournier*.

We were in a group of ten professional persons. I was the only minister. There were two bankers. There was a lawyer. There were three salesmen. There was one accountant. An explosives expert (Don't ask!). And the leader, a management consultant. One of the bankers was speaking in response to a statement I had just made.

"You have no idea what it is like," he said. "We have to do the same thing over and over." He was making gesturing signs with his hands and arms, circular motions. "It is boring, boring, boring. There is no letup. The pressure is constant, and the variety is virtually nil." He was inferring that the ministry is not at all like that. In most cases it is not. There are some hints of truth in this statement, though, even for the minister. Sometimes, he can get bored. Sometimes he feels that the ministry is doing the same thing over and over. He wants to maintain that high energy level and high excitement intensity of ministry. It is often difficult.

What can the minister do to maintain the high level of excitement in his professional life? How can he know when his professional skills need honing? When is it time for the minister to attend a continuing education program, a conference, a workshop, or some kind of training event which will help him to resensitize his professional life?

WHAT IS BURNOUT IN THE MINISTER'S PROFESSIONAL LIFE?

At its very worst, burnout occurs when there is really nothing that the person cares about. He goes to his work without any symptoms of optimism. Negative feelings consume the thought processes. He feels depressed. He doesn't really want to be around the people he works with, but the strange part of it is he doesn't want to be away from people all that much either. Nothing satisfies his wants and needs. He feels torn apart. He begins to treat people in a dehumanizing way. They are simply a necessary part of getting through the day. Compassion is difficult if not impossible.

He feels put down by others. He feels put upon by persons who seek favors or who want something from him. He begins to feel so used that he suspects others only do him favors for what they can get out of him at a later time.

Many feel that the reason the television series *M*A*S*H*, starring Alan Alda and others, is a continuing hit is because it depicts a group of people who have learned to cope with burnout with humor. Somehow their ability to cope gives the viewing public some hope that they, too, can learn to cope with their own burnout. Joseph Wambaugh's harsh and unpleasant novel, *The Choirboys*, is also a story of a group of persons who cope with burnout by alcohol, dope, and sex. These persons, the medical profession in *M*A*S*H*, and the policemen in *The Choirboys*, are coping in ways that are socially and morally unacceptable for the minister. The minister cannot expect to obliterate authority in the same manner as the actors in *M*A*S*H*. They certainly cannot expect to keep their jobs if they use the same strategies as the cops in *The Choirboys*. Then what can they do? What are the choices?

(1) Snobs

Some become intellectually *snobbish*. They rise above all the mundane tasks of ministry. They do not feel the need to bow to the neurotic demands of unreasonable church members. They resume their student role (some at the ages of 40's and 50's) and become absorbed in academic theology rather than the practical application of biblical theology. They take what some people call a "head trip." Somehow, they feel this immunizes them from the dirty business of "paying the rent." "Paying the rent" is a phrase for meeting the expectations of those persons who examine the job description of the minister from time to time.

(2) Suitors

Some ministers become *suitors*. They are not the kind of suitors who pursue persons of the opposite sex. These ministers pursue pulpit committees and others who are influential in churches. They court them with clever and subtle techniques that only another minister would understand. They work through their friends and acquaintances to make the contact with the pulpit committee and/or church. They spend much of their energies discussing the possibility of going to another church, and often a particular church that is pastorless.

At the beginning of this subtopic, the phrase, "At its very worst . . ." was used. Most ministers do not deliberately set out to become intellectual snobs or suitors of churches with vacant pulpits. The culprit is their own professional vacuum. It is not a life-style. It is more a stage of their profession. After all, life is not a *state*, it is a movement. Even those who adopt some of these patterns, for the most part, have integrity. It is difficult to admit that we all somehow fall into these practices in some way or other.

(3) Exhaustion

So then what is burnout in the professional life of the minister? In its most abbreviated form, it is *exhaustion*. Sometimes the exhaustion is emotional, sometimes physical; sometimes spiritual. In the professional realm it takes on the form of exhaustion which causes us to stop growing. When we stop growing, we are in trouble.

Gary R. Collins developed a brief instrument to determine whether one has professional burnout.

ARE YOU BURNED OUT?[1]

For each statement, circle whether this is rarely true (R) in your life, sometimes true (S) or usually true (U)

```
R  S  U
0  1  2  I feel exhausted and run down
0  1  2  I am irritable
0  1  2  I get frustrated easily
0  1  2  I feel helpless
0  1  2  I have trouble sleeping
0  1  2  I am discouraged
0  1  2  I tend to be critical of others
0  1  2  I tend to be critical of myself
0  1  2  I want to get away from people
0  1  2  I would like to change my job
0  1  2  I feel spiritually dull
0  1  2  I think that my job is stressful
0  1  2  I feel under constant pressure
0  1  2  I have difficulty being with troubled people
```

0   1   2   I am impatient
0   1   2   I lack enthusiasm

(If you scored in the range of 16-32 points, you may be a victim of burnout.)

GETTING A GRIP ON THE DOWN SIDE

One minister commented, "I am just going through the motions. I remember when it was fun to go to the office and get a good view of the day. I would visit and witness. I prepared by day and worked and participated by night. Now, it seems everyone I witness to has a way of making me feel put down. It did not bother me when I started. It certainly does now."

(1) Depression

When the professional side of the minister is affected by burnout, he feels depressed. Depression is a normal part of living. But the minister is not supposed to be depressed. He is supposed to help others deal with their depression. It is not only shocking to his church members when they find their minister is fighting depression, it is shocking to the minister himself.

Many studies prove that the more successful a person is the more likely he is to be depressed. If this is true for the general population, then it is true for the minister. In fact, Ronald R. Fieve, MD, a psychiatrist from New York City and author of *Moodswing, The Third Revolution in Psychiatry* (Bantam, 1976) "estimates that between 15 and 20 percent of the adult population suffers from some form of depression."[2] He calls depression an "illness of success."[3]

Why is success so depressing? "For the same reason failure is: It's a source of stress. It forces us to look at who we are, where we are going, why we are going—and whether or not we deserve to be going. If it makes you feel any better, Abraham Lincoln, Theodore Roosevelt and Winston Churchill all had recurrent bouts with depression."[4]

Now, let us look at that reasoning in the light of ministry. Suppose a minister has been super successful as a youth evangelist. He has seen persons saved. He has watched a church become revived. He has felt the response to his youthful zest in ministry and had visions of Billy Graham greatness in his repertoire of vocational hopes. All of a sudden, he finds himself forty-five years of age, and the pastor of a church that seems to be going nowhere. Where is the fire he lit some twenty years ago? Where is his zest for living? Where has the need for being in front of people preaching to throngs gone? He may be successful to the people in his church, but is he successful in comparison with his peers? His concept of success in ministry must fall under close scrutiny. If it does not measure up, then it is predictable that he will feel the pains of depression.

(2) Pitstop

How can the minister get a grip on this down side of his professional life? How about viewing it as a *pitstop*? Most of my friends who are ministers deny the feeling of depression brought on by disappointments in their professional life. If we could relieve the guilt about this one area by seeing it as a *pitstop*, then perhaps we could view the whole subject with more objectivity.

A *pitstop* is a place to refuel. It is necessary for survival. It is a place where we can "prepare" to bounce back. Privacy and isolation alone are not the answer. Often privacy and isolation increase rather than decrease the problem. Purposeful privacy and purposeful isolation can help. Design the privacy so that we know what the privacy is for.

Jesus had begun his mission. He had already faced the wiles of the devil. He had been rejected at Nazareth; he had driven out an evil spirit in Capernaum, and was healing persons who were brought to him. Luke tells a beautiful part of Jesus' ministry where he felt the need for refueling.

When the sun was setting, the people brought to Jesus all who had various kinds of sickness, and laying his hands on each one, he healed them. Moreover, demons came out of many people, shouting, "You are the Son of God!" But he rebuked them and would not allow them to speak, because they knew he was the Christ. At daybreak Jesus went out to a solitary place (Luke 4:40-42, NIV).

He went out where the poeple could not find him. They had to search for him. The first time I found this passage it was as if an insurmountable weight of guilt had been lifted from me. It would not be the last time Jesus would seek out a place to be alone with God. He needed the refueling as we all do. All persons who serve God and try to meet the needs of persons must have a pitstop now and then if they are to survive.

YOU CAN PROGRAM FAILURE

It is possible to program your own failure. It is even more possible for the keenly interested and competent person in the area of human behavior, vis a vis, the minister. He has a head start. He is intrigued with the way the mind and feelings work. He is analytical and finds some kind of recreation in describing the many facets of pain. When his own burnout occurs, he laments, "Yeah, I knew it was coming. I could see the symptoms." Somehow, in his own mind *he has excused it by explaining it.*

When I first became involved in the area of pastoral care, I could concentrate on very little else. I was in love with the idea of being able to describe the many ways people hurt. I found myself playing amateur psychologist with almost everyone I communicated with. That included my wife and the members of the church where I was pastor.

One of the most memorable experiences was with a deacon named Gordon. Gordon was giving me fits. I could expect some kind of crisis from him almost every Sunday. He found loopholes in every leadership move I made. He was constantly (so it seemed to me) finding fault with the way our worship experience was being conducted. I became deeply engrossed in my second pastoral care course and was becoming "expert" because I had had the introductory course. I did my exploratory interview with Gordon under the guise of discussing a problem he was having with a biblical passage. I found out he was married a second time. His first wife had died unexpectedly with a heart attack. He had not worked through the grief process. In fact, his denial was so strong that he picked up with her life process in another woman and married his wife again, although she was an entirely different person than he thought she was. He thought he had found a woman exactly like the first. He would not allow the second wife to become anything but what his first wife was. When she began to show signs of individuality after three years of marriage (they were both in their early 50's), he became angry at the world. Why would she not be Edith, his first wife? Maybe it was the pastor's fault. After all, he is the representative of God. He is the one who speaks in behalf of God. And God had done this injustice. His guilt would not let him be angry at God, therefore he could comfortably take it out on the pastor (that was me).

After this brilliant revelation, I was overjoyed. I discussed it with my colleagues and supervisor and they concurred. What else could they do? I had become skilled in analysis in just my third year in seminary. Then the problem began. I knew how to theorize what was wrong, but I did not know how to interpret it to Gordon. Nor did I know how to deal with the situation redemptively. Being able to identify this complex problem was interesting, and it did require a great deal of skill (of which I am still proud), but it did not solve the conflict with Gordon. For several weeks I tried to act out the possible solutions with Gordon. Nothing seemed to work. In fact, things seemed to get worse. I began to feel guilt. The whole situation was more than I could deal with. Then I began to feel failure. I had programmed my own failure. A little information was helpful. A lot of information would have been much more helpful. I did not have a lot of information. I had gotten in over my head. I had enough to feel miserable. I was becoming skilled at a very primitive level of psychotherapy. I was at a loss to know what to do with a person who had become deeply disturbed emotionally. Eventually, he was hospitalized and found some professional help. I can honestly say I have worked through much of my own feelings of failure and guilt but there is still a part of that experience that reminds me of what I have still to learn. I felt I had programmed my own failure by knowing a little . . . but not enough.

This experience gives me the sensible assurance that it is possible to program my own failure. If I do so to an exaggerated extent, then I will certainly affect my vocational burnout. I must keep my professional edge growing along with my spiritual edge. I must continue to know that I cannot set my sights so high that I cannot reach them.

There is still some gamesmanship in identifying the types of emotional problems that are present in church members. I often find myself finding some satisfaction in explaining to myself, "The reason he is acting that way is because he had a domineering father and an overprotective mother. Surely, he is entitled to act that way because of these detriments to his emotional growth and well-being." At other times, I say, "He or she is lacking in self-esteem. They are overly critical because they look down on themselves."

. . . But I try to stop myself before I program my own failure. I have definite limits in my skills. I want to remind myself that I may have the skills to identify some of the more complex problems, but I also must not program myself into thinking that I can solve them all. With God's help, and his active grace, many of the problems in man's emotional and spiritual life can be solved. But I am only one instrument among a great number of instruments. If I begin to play God with my skills, I have programmed myself for definite failure. The same is true for any minister who works with people. He cannot be all things to all people, even though Paul's admonition is great preaching and an admirable pursuit.

THE 3-D THEORY OF AVOIDING PROFESSIONAL BURNOUT

A minister wants to fulfill his call. He feels a sense of mission if he is worth his salt. And, I am only writing to those who feel a sense of mission.

After feeling a call to ministry, he begins preparation for his mission. He studies to show himself approved. He wants to be a workman for God without shame. He wants to be an effective minister. When and if he does begin to feel some sense of burnout then he certainly wants to do something about it. I believe there is a practical formula that will help. I call it the 3-D theory of avoiding professional burnout in ministry. Picture three concentric circles. One cannot exist without the other two. They are interlinked. One is **mission**. Two is **demands**. Three is **fulfillment**. The three functional images help the minister avoid burnout.

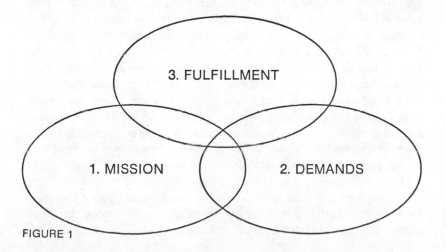

FIGURE 1

(1) Mission

The first part of the 3-D view of the personal image of ministry is mission. He must know what he is about. He must know what he wants out of his ministry.

There is at least a two part view of mission. There is first that part of our calling that we would like to *be* ourselves. It may not be clear to us when we accept the call into ministry. In other words, we may be unclear about whether God is calling us into a pastoral role, a minister of education, or missionary role. There are multiple numbers of specific roles that we may choose as a result of becoming what God wants us to be. We will make these choices as we discover our gifts. As we prepare educationally, the picture becomes much more clear. We begin to find ourselves more comfortable in some of our work in ministry than in other parts.

Still complicating the role of mission even more is that many change roles in ministry during the pilgrimage. Keeping the focus of our mission is imperative to functional peace.

The second part of our mission is that which we would like to do with our role in ministry. We must decide where we are to do our ministry. We must decide when and where we will do our mission. We must choose how well prepared we are to do our mission. In making choices, this means we must choose how much and what kind of educational preparation is necessary for us to do our mission. Some will begin their mission by "doing" immediately. These ministers feel they are prepared as soon as they are called. Many of these persons made excellent servants of God's mission just as did many of the less educated persons during New Testament times. Jesus chose the common and simple men and women of his time to do his mission. The pattern is still true today. Others, however, know that it is essential for them to prepare themselves more thoroughly. They go on to college. They acquire a seminary degree. Some continue until they have completed their doctor's degree. These persons are preparing themselves because they see preparation as a part of "doing" their mission.

Doing our mission also includes where. We are often inclined to do our mission in the state from which we have come. Some choose a foreign land. Some choose a pioneer area. Some choose an urban setting. Still others choose a rural setting.

Being and doing are the measurements of our own mission. If we continue with incentive to be what God wants us to be and do what God wants us to do, we will have the momentum necessary to combat burnout in ministry.

The story is told of a junior officer in the Navy who was impressed with the overwhelming zeal of his commanding officer. He watched his commanding officer go with enthusiasm and vigor long after everyone else seemed to tire. When the junior officer questioned the commanding officer about his desire to serve, he responded, "I care about this ship. To be Captain means that I am responsible. I have worked long and hard to be Captain. I have paid my dues. I take great pride in what I am and in what I do. It comes out of my desire to serve." I believe this commanding officer had a mission. He knew what he wanted to be and he knew what he wanted to do. The ship can be analogous to our church. The commanding officer can be analogous to any minister in any church (as long as he doesn't take the authority of a commanding officer too seriously).

(2) Demands

The second part of the 3-D theory of preservation of ministry from burnout in his vocation is understanding the demands on ministry. More specifically, it is understanding the demands on the minister himself.

At this stage, it is with candor and realism that the minister must look at his strengths and weaknesses. He must know what is demanded of him, and he must know how capable he is of fulfilling these demands.

One of the more frustrating parts of my pastoral ministry was trying to meet the expectations of those persons who wanted a "weekly" pastoral visit. Some deserved to be visited each week. These persons were in need of pastoral care. Some were near death. Others were terminally ill. These persons did not bother me. I visited them gladly. Others did bother me. It was the semi-invalid member who would pout for several weeks if the pastoral visit did not meet his or her expectations. I found myself resenting "paying the rent" of visiting those who expected me to visit them. I would fight myself from being sarcastic or less than compassionate. I played games with myself in order to meet the reasonable demands.

Other parts of my ministry made demands which were met with less reluctance. I enjoyed the demands of preparation. The discipline of preparing three "fresh" messages a week was a favorite part of my work. I enjoyed the demands of hospital visitation. Even though it often posed a hardship financially because of the multiple hospitals used by the membership, it still remained a favorite part of the ministry which I considered to be demanding.

Understanding the demands and understanding one's own abilities to meet the demands can preserve much energy. One question that should be posed at this juncture is: Do I prefer to do things myself, or do I prefer to help others to get things done? This is more than delegation. This is the willingness to be satisfied with getting the job done . . . even when I don't do it myself. Some ministers find that doing a job on their own is much more satisfying than training someone else to do the job and watching them as they do it. "If you want something done right, you have to do it yourself," is a favorite comment by these persons who minister to the demands of his church's mission.

A favorite pastime of motivational experts is arguing the case of whether it is better to spend more time in correcting your weaknesses or to spend more time in sharpening your strengths and skills. The issue of which is better is far from settled. It is my opinion that a minister will burn out quicker if he spends most of his energy on trying to correct his weaknesses. It sounds like an honorable way to go about meeting the demands, but it is also exhausting. If he spends his major energies on correcting his weaknesses, he is using some negative energy. He begins with the premise that he is not what he should be and is trying to become what he should be. Some of this attitude is not only admirable but it is essential. Too much of this attitude will tell on him eventually. For example, he does not enjoy preparation for preaching, but he does enjoy preaching. He enjoys being in front of his congregation. He does not enjoy so much being in the study preparing to be in front of his congregation. In an effort to correct his weakness, he disciplines himself to spend more time in the study. He does so. But he finds himself doing more of the same. He is spending the time but he is not preparing himself better. The reason may be very simple. He may be spinning his wheels. He is there but he is not there. He is in the office and behind the desk but his study habits are so laborious that he does not prepare well for what he is doing.

George McIntyre, head football coach at Vanderbilt University, told a chapel audience recently that he had no idea how much work went into a two-hour period on Saturday afternoon while he was watching football before he started playing. The real labor to make a good football player is Monday through Friday practices. Draw the analogy for the pastor in the pulpit on Sunday.

It is not as simplistic as it seems, but there is a way to meet the demands more easily without burning out so quickly. Assuming the demands he feels are in sermon preparation, why not search for the sermon idea wherever he feels comfortable? He may find more pleasure in visiting the lost. He could begin the germinating process while he is doing what he enjoys doing . . . witnessing to the lost. He does not have to feel guilty for not preparing himself better. He could find the idea and begin to make notes wherever he is. He could then search for the resources as his sermon idea builds and develops. He could carry a notebook to take notes in the process. Rather than spending three hours of disciplined time in the study, he would be spending three hours over the course of a day and a half, at fifteen minute intervals. He may find himself better prepared than if he had spent the entire three hours in straight time. This would be a way of developing his strengths and spending more energy on where he is best and in the process correct a weakness without becoming angry about feeling forced to meet the demands of study.

Monitoring can be the minister's best friend in meeting the demands in ministry. "Monitoring" is taking stock of how you are meeting the demands. "Monitoring" is listening to what you are doing.

There are many ways to monitor. Monitoring can be done with the help of a friend, or a wife or husband.

It can be done with dispatch and organization, or it can be done informally.

One minister has a Monday lunch with the director of the Sunday School and the chairman of deacons each week. These persons evaluate the attendance, the spirit of the preceding Sunday, and the balance of the worship experience. Each man has an opportunity to give his evaluation of the previous day's experiences. The minister encourages the two men to give him feedback about his two sermons. He has met with them long enough that they do not feel compelled to tell him just what he wants to hear. They often tell him more than he wants to hear. He feels that the Monday lunch is one of the best exercises in monitoring his progress and effectiveness in ministry that he has tried.

Another church staff has a rap session each Monday morning from

9:00 until 11:00 AM. During this rap session, each member evaluates the mood and temperament of the services on the previous Sunday. A creative devotional experience is planned for each Monday morning. Recognizing that the Sunday is planned to meet the needs of the church members, the church staff knows that their own needs for spiritual nourishment must be met. Since they are responsible for leading the worship experiences for the church members, they plan to have a very special devotional experience for themselves. The church staff concurs that the experience has helped to integrate the spiritual dimension of life with other experiences. It also gives them an opportunity to "monitor" their spiritual needs out of the context of the entire church. It helps them to avoid being anesthetized to the awesomeness of worship.

The minister must know the territory if he is to meet the demands of his church. In this arena, tradition plays an important part. If the tradition of the church has been for the pastor to visit in regular intervals a specific segment of the church membership, and the arriving new minister decides to change this tradition, he may be inviting a culture shock. It is essential that he know what territorial boundaries are in the expectations of those church members who legitimize the attitude toward the pastor. He should introduce radically different approaches slowly rather than abruptly, if at all.

I can almost hear a good friend of mine respond, "Hey, Faulkner, that's politics, pure and simple!" And I would have to say, "You're probably right!"

Politics is a rather dirty word to many. It is also a reality the minister must face if he wishes to meet the demands of his profession.

Some church members legitimize much of the action and movement of a church. These persons are frequently less vocal than most. These are the persons who are consulted when the problem is sticky or thorny. It may be the one or two persons who very rarely speak out in a business meeting. A simple nod or even virtual silence may give approval or disapproval. Then along comes the proverbial "bull in the china shop" leader who feels, "No one is going to tell me what to do!" He may even take definite steps to contradict these legitimizers and go against the grain of the movement of the church. These ministers often win the battles of the moment. They also frequently lose the wars of effectiveness in the long run.

Knowing the territory is a part of meeting the demands. Knowing who the legitimizers are is a part of getting to know the territory. It is a logical process. It is also a fun process if the leader does not allow himself to become threatened by the power of persuasiveness of the legitimizers. As a friend, the legitimizer will help him get his work done much more fluidly and quickly.

At least two kinds of legitimizers exist in a church. There is the legitimizer who feels that he (or she) must have a voice in every decision. These persons build their own power networks and loyalists. Around these persons, it is wise to tread carefully and softly. The second kind of legitimizer is the person who is truly a wise and caring person who has grown to be trusted by others because of his or her wisdom and compassion. I have found these persons to be friends to the mission of the church and the ministry of the pastor. I have also found some of my best support systems in these persons. They do not need the power that is given them. They have had the power thrust upon them. Through the years, they have grown to feel the weight of the welfare of the church and have acted responsibly.

(3) Fulfillment

The third part of the 3-D theory of managing burnout in the professional life of the minister is fulfillment. He must find ways to be fulfilled as a person if he is to continue to be effective in his life.

To be fulfilled, one must know what his goals are and how he or she is progressing toward accomplishing these goals. It is only natural that a minister wants his church to grow. If he begins to establish practical means for helping his church to grow, then it is natural to expect to be able to see the progress. If he does not see the progress, it is difficult for him to feel the fulfillment necessary.

Achievement is one measure of fulfillment. If he feels he has achieved, he can be fulfilled. Achievement is measured in many different ways. Increasing attendance in Sunday School or Church Training is one measure of achievement. Winning people to Christ is another measure of achievement. Many lay persons in churches have grown to expect the minister to be responsible for winning people to Christ. If there are a measurable number of decisions, these persons feel the minister is "producing." If the number of decisions for Christ is limited, then these persons assume the minister is "not producing."

I am frequently encouraged to remember the pilgrimage of Adoniram Judson who spent several years in Burma before winning the first person to Christ. This is not an excuse for those ministers who do not try to win people to Christ. This is an encouragement to those who try but feel that they have failed because there is very little measure of persons who have made decisions for Christ.

Perhaps we need more Johnny Appleseed type ministers. Johnny Appleseed, so the legend goes, went all over the new world planting apple trees. He did not enjoy the fruits of the labors himself. He was satisfied for others to gather the fruit. He found joy in planting trees.

The first church I pastored was Mid City Baptist Church. I was barely seventeen years old. I knew very little about winning people to Christ. I knew even less about how to preach an effective sermon. In January, I became pastor of Mid City, a church located between Kennett and Hayti, Missouri. There were five persons present. In a few weeks we were running well over 100 in Sunday School. We were having decisions for Christ weekly. I began to believe that I was a remarkable evangelist. By August, our church was booming. I had thoroughly convinced myself that I was going to become famous as a preacher. It was during the year following that I learned the truth about what was really going on in Mid City Baptist Church. Oma Risener was a member of Mid City Baptist Church. She and Sam, her husband, Carla and Reba, their daughters, were four of the five persons present back on that cold January Sunday morning. She adopted me. She prayed for me. She visited during the week while I was still in high school. She won people to Christ. She believed in me. While I would preach on Sunday morning, during the week before Sunday she would have people ready to make decisions when the invitation was given. She trained others to win people to Christ. They, in turn, continued to make me look good. I was achieving because it was measurable.

The following year, upon entrance in Southwest Baptist College, in Bolivar, Missouri, I became pastor of High Point Baptist Church, near Bolivar. (The preacher was the same, even some of the sermons were the same.) The enthusiasm was the same. *But the results were quite different.* During the first year of my ministry at High Point, we had only one decision for Christ. All of a sudden, I was a failure. I was not the greatest evangelist on earth. I was not even good. My measurement for achievement was woefully lacking. I knew I had to find other ways to make myself useful than to measure my effectiveness by the number of decisions I was having each Sunday. It was during this year of "failure" that I began to realize how valuable people like Oma Risener were to the effectiveness of my ministry.

For me, there had to be more to fulfillment than the criterion of achievement I used that first year.

One way I've found to broaden the span of fulfillment is to broaden my dreams. I began to feel a sense of fulfillment when I had accomplished the first step in my educational process. I received an Associate of Arts degree from Bolivar's Southwest Baptist College. At the time, it was a Junior College. I knew my next step was to finish a bachelor's degree. I did so at Southeast Missouri State University, in Cape Girardeau, Missouri. I felt that my educational preparation would prepare me for the task of ministry. The educational pilgrimage continued through The Southern Baptist Theological Seminary in Louisville, Kentucky.

I found satisfaction in serving in other staff positions. I became minister of music (also custodian) at College Street Baptist Church in Springfield, Missouri, while enrolled at Southwest Baptist College. Later I became associate pastor at the First Baptist Church in Caruthersville, Missouri. I found a great deal of fulfillment in experimenting and at the same time serving in staff positions.

Still other forms of fulfillment came in knowing I had a part in making things happen. Technically, it is called administrative skills. Emotionally, it is simply getting things done and enjoying the feeling of knowing it.

But the greatest fulfillment in my ministry was in being a part of helping people through times of crisis and stress. The grief process for any church member is painful. The minister can help a church member work through that grief process. The feeling of caring for others is irreplaceable. I felt most fulfilled when I was a part of moving people through the grief process. If I could help a young mother and father work through the pain of losing a son who had been taken by cancer, I was doing a part of what I had been called to do . . . to lend comfort to those in pain.

And, as time passes, the ways of being fulfilled change. After serving as pastor of Faith Baptist Church in Georgetown, Kentucky, Howard Foshee and Bill Young of the Church Administration Department of the Baptist Sunday School Board contacted me about the possibility of serving as a consultant in that department. I used my pastoral skills. Later, when my years of being a consultant reached a plateau, I wanted to exercise my skills as a manager. It took several efforts to convince my superiors that I was ready and able. The opportunity was finally given me by Reggie McDonough, who is now Associate Executive Secretary-Treasurer of the Executive Committee of the Southern Baptist Convention. At the time he was the secretary of the Church Administration Department. For the past three years, my fulfillment has been most recognized (by me, at least) in being a manager. I have been supervisor of the Career Guidance Section of the Church Administration Department. The ways of finding fulfillment have changed dramatically during the twenty-eight years of my ministry. Also, my concept of achievement has changed.

A progressive way of finding the times in your patterns of ministry that give fulfillment has been suggested by a recent book by Bernard Haldane, *Career Satisfaction and Success*. Although Haldane suggested a number of items which are applicable to the manager and leader of today, we have selected only those we felt most pertinent to the role of the minister.

a. "Design, color, or shape things"

When a minister explores his strengths for the express purpose of using them to find fulfillment, he should look at his own need to "design, color, or shape things."[5] This is a part of the artistic nature of persons. In theology, we studied the *creatio ex nihilo* concept of God's power. God is the only being who is able to create something out of nothing. All others create out of something which has already been created. Man finds fulfillment by creating out of something. To do this he designs, colors, or shapes things. He puts his own imprint on an item which already exists. Although there have been many magnificent preachers, the minister who feels that only he can preach with the expertise which he possesses is preaching with his own identity. He is designing, or coloring, or shaping things which are already in existence. When he is convinced that he has designed a sermon like only he can design a sermon, it is natural that he would feel fulfillment from this creative endeavor.

b. "Observe, operate, or inspect"

Another suggestion in landscaping one's strengths is to "observe, operate, or inspect."[6] Not many see what really goes on around them. Those who do are special. These are those unique individuals who are perceptive to the point of knowing when some things make a difference. The opposite of this use of skills is to become bored or blind to the influences of one's surroundings. *Observation* is one way of knowing that your ministry is making a difference in the lives of the persons to whom you give your life. *Operation* is the ability to conduct oneself in a way which changes things. *Inspecting* is the skill of feedback. Inspection can be given to one's own set of values or it can be given to those with whom we work.

c. "Write, read, talk, speak, or teach"

Haldane lumps the following together, "write, read, talk, speak, and teach."[7] Perhaps the reason he does it is because each of the five words suggests some form of communication. If the minister does not feel good in his ability to write, read, talk, speak, or teach, he is already in deep trouble. If he does feel good about these abilities, then it is natural that he would want to improve them. In improving, he is measuring his own source of fulfillment.

d. "Analyze, systematize, research"

Others find fulfillment in their ability to "analyze, systematize, research."[8] These are the problem-solving skills. If a minister is leading a planning group in deciding the building needs of the church, he will get a great deal of satisfaction in sharing his skills in analyzing the needs of the congregation which brought them to the point of deciding why they should build. These ministers get good feelings from leading a group to visit other churches to explore the sizes and shapes of buildings and how these buildings met the needs of other churches.

It may be important to note that many ministers feel "burned out" immediately following a large building program. I have heard the phrase, "I believe the Lord is leading me to another church. I have completed my mission here." Perhaps he is saying that he has thoroughly enjoyed being able to use his analytical, systematizing, and research skills. He would like to be able to continue to use these skills. Since the church has completed the building program, he does not see that these particular skills will be used again right away.

e. "Invent, develop, create, and imagine"

Continuing, there are the "invent, develop, create, and imagine"[9] skills. These skills result in the production of books, or in the case of the minister who is a preacher, the production of sermons, or new ideas which have meaning. These skills also lead to constructive changes which take place in churches, and in the life of the minister himself. There is a constant demand for creative people, but not all churches welcome creative people in the same way. Those who make noises of being creative are often greeted with some caution, and maybe even suspicion. Some tread softly. Others barge in and find more than they have bargained for, to the point of thwarting their effectiveness.

Some ministers must have their creative skills exercised. These are the persons who are not content to feel that changes have been dramatic when a shift in the order of worship has been made. These ministers feel that dramatic changes must be made often. Organizations must be changed. Floor plans must be changed. Visitation programs must be changed. Personnel must be changed. Committees and deacons must be rotated. The fulfillment for these types of persons comes when the complexion of the church no longer looks like it did when the former minister was in the church. In fact, these persons may be measuring their effectiveness based on their ability to "change" things. It is disturbing for them to finally recognize that change does not necessarily mean that they have been creative. Sometimes keeping things as they are is more creative than changing things.

f. "Help people, be of service, be kind"

"Help people, be of service, be kind"[10] is the skill of human and personal relations. Every minister who has been called of God must have the arena to exercise his or her compassion skills. Occupations which help people are not enough. The minister must help people in a particular way. He must help people find Christ as personal Savior. He must be of service in a specific problem of death, or disturbance, or difficulty. He must know that he is able to give kindness in a meaningful way to the people who seek the guidance and counsel of Christ.

Paul wrote to the Ephesians "Be kind and compassionate to one another, forgiving each other, just as in Christ God forgave you" (Eph. 4:32, NIV). Ministers, to find fulfillment, must take this admonition seriously. Just as a baseball player cannot be effective without a baseball and a glove, the minister cannot be effective without kindness and compassion. Lay persons will forgive the minister of most any deficiency (even preaching poorly) in the tools of his trade except these.

Swan Haworth, a notable minister of compassion and a professor of pastoral care at The Southern Baptist Theological Seminary at the time of the incident, was in Oklahoma to participate in a Church Staff/Relations Conference for churches with multiple staffs. An instrument of detecting personal relations skills was used in the conference, a FIRO-B (Fundamentals of Interpersonal Relations Orientation-Behavior). One minister who was a participant found himself disgruntled with the findings. After several leading questions by the minister to Dr. Haworth about the validity of the instrument, he asked if Dr. Haworth thought that he (the minister) were as poor in relating to people as the instrument indicated. "If I were you, I would certainly want to look at why I was in the ministry, if that instrument is true." The other participants did not laugh. Neither did the questioning minister. It was a profound statement. If a minister is not in the business of liking people, if he did not want to help, be of service, and find satisfaction in being kind, he needs to look at *why* he is in the ministry.

    g. "Manage or direct others"

"Manage or direct others."[11] The comment did not pass by me lightly. A friend was attending a pastoral leadership seminar at the Church Program Training Center in Nashville, Tennessee. "Faulkner, I wish I had your job," he said, and continued, "that way I wouldn't have to work, just boss people around." It was not amusing. He did not understand what it means to manage people. I am not sure I do.

    This skill could be tagged the leadership item in this list of items which bring fulfillment to the minister. Leadership is an enigma. It is impossible to define. Even when it can be identified, it will change. Effective leadership today will be ineffective leadership tomorrow. You and I both know ministers who have been pastors for twenty-five years in the same church, and then one Sunday, a group of powerful and influential deacons decide that his effectiveness is no longer in evidence. He is asked to resign. He has been effective for years but suddenly, without warning, these persons do not feel that he is effective any longer. Right or wrong, the concept of effective leadership has changed.

    Leadership is often identified as the ability to influence people to get things done. It also includes the ability to help people to grow personally. Managing and directing others can be an ego trip if it is not in keeping with this dimension of leadership. Managing is anything but "bossing people around." Managing is to serve those to whom you are responsible. Managing is helping others to do and be what is right both for the manager and the worker.

    Managing or directing others includes persuading others to get their own goals and objectives into focus. When the activity or event is finished, the church members should be able to feel that they themselves have accomplished something. Good management does just that. It helps them to accomplish, and then gives them credit for it.

    h. "Performance"

One other skill should be considered in this list of items which are considered in fulfillment: "performance."[12] Some ministers are better than others at getting up before others and performing. Some measure their effectiveness by their ability to "perform."

Performance would include both *proclamation* and *teaching*. It would include musical performance, acting, drama, and demonstrations. Some ministers of music are evaluated solely on the basis of their performance skills. Satisfaction can come only when they feel they have performed well. Some ministers are depressed for two days following what they consider a poor showing in the sermon. They have performed poorly. But also good performance can produce good feelings. If the feedback has been positive, then they can thrive on these strokes for a couple of days. Performance is important but it is not the only measure of effectiveness.

In this chapter on burnout in the professional life of the minister, we have sought to recognize the symptoms of burnout. We have sought to define burnout in the minister's professional life. We have used instruments to determine the extent of burnout. We have made some suggestions on how to get a grip on the down side of burnout. We have discussed how some ministers actually program their own failure by setting their goals higher than they are able to achieve.

The heart of the chapter has been in a definition of the 3-D theory of avoiding professional burnout. The three portions of this theory are recognizing the (1) *Mission* of the minister; (2) Dealing with the *Demands* of the minister; and (3) Dealing with the areas of *Fulfillment* in the minister.

Since the subtitle of this book is "How to Recognize it; How to Avoid It," most of the content has been aimed at identifying the practical applications of overcoming burnout as opposed to simply trying to define it.

In the next chapter, we will deal with the physical symptoms of burnout in the minister's life.

4

Burnout in the Minister's Physical Life

Like a tree each of us must have room to grow . . . to branch out. We are dependent on the elements for sustenance—to God for inner strength to combat the uncontrollable elements—to ourselves for response to the gift of physical recreative processes.

"Our pastor is a great preacher. He's just too fat!"

"I took my pastor to the Kiwanis Club, and to tell you the truth, I was ashamed of him. He had stains all over his tie. He was dressed with white socks and a black suit. He acted like he just didn't care how he looked. He has never been that way before. He used to be the best dressed man in our community."

"Our pastor's relationship to the church has turned into an arrangement. He is not the dynamic leader he used to be. He has no set hours at the office. He can neither be reached at his home. He has lost all interest in golf and tennis, and he used to be one of the most avid golfers in town."

You are listening to the stories of three ministers whose physical lives have taken on signs and signals of burnout. What has happened to them?

Certain danger signs occur when the minister begins to feel physical burnout. (See Figure 2.)

(1) *He begins to feel tired frequently.*

His body does not work like it should. He finds himself comparing his life to earlier years. He reasons that he used to be able to pop out of bed and begin the day with vigor and vitality. Now it takes a while for the blood to get pumping. He can no longer establish an energy level that will last all day.

Even the times during the day when he feels rested don't last long.

59

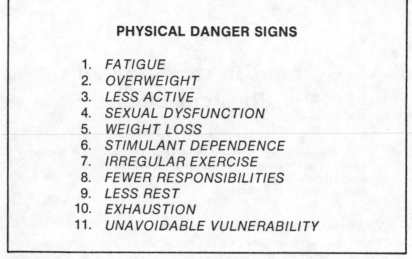

PHYSICAL DANGER SIGNS

 1. *FATIGUE*
 2. *OVERWEIGHT*
 3. *LESS ACTIVE*
 4. *SEXUAL DYSFUNCTION*
 5. *WEIGHT LOSS*
 6. *STIMULANT DEPENDENCE*
 7. *IRREGULAR EXERCISE*
 8. *FEWER RESPONSIBILITIES*
 9. *LESS REST*
10. *EXHAUSTION*
11. *UNAVOIDABLE VULNERABILITY*

FIGURE 2

He begins to look forward to the times when he can rest without feeling guilty.

(2) *He begins to gain weight.*

A certain amount of weight gain is normal. But the minister who continues to gain weight when his frame could be a healthy specimen with a little more effort usually has a more serious problem than the normal gaining of a few pounds.

He begins to change sizes of pants frequently. He goes from a 32″ to a 36″ in six months. Then six months later he has gone to a 38″ waist. His coat size has changed from a size Regular 40 to a Size 44 in just one year. Nothing fits that fitted him two years ago.

He finds excuses to take snacks to eat between meals. He arranges more than his share of snacks to watch television.

(3) *He spends fewer hours at previously favorite activities.*

Life gets tedious. Things become boring. Activities are nerve-racking. Or he is simply not able to keep his attention centered for any length of time. He finds it difficult to relax while doing some of the things he used to enjoy doing. His body does not function in the ways which make things enjoyable. The consequence is that he does more and more things with less and less satisfaction. His functional body activities just don't allow for the gratification they once did.

(4) *His sexual energies have waned.*

He may have become completely impotent. Perhaps it has scared him so much that he has failed to talk to anyone about it . . . including his physician. He may have some of the old-fashioned ideas of manliness tied up with his sexual energies. He finds it difficult even to talk to his wife. One pastor suggested, "How can I explain my embarrassment to my wife when I can't explain it to myself?"

It is difficult for some ministers to realize that the same physical changes take place in him as take place in those he tries to explain physical changes to in his membership. Many of us have made ourselves believe that we are immune to the same problems we try to minister to in our congregation. Sexual energies will change. If the change is alarming, consult a physician.

(5) *He begins to lose weight.*

Just as serious as gaining weight is the problem of losing weight at the rate of inordinate or unplanned stages. He finds himself finding more and more excuses for not eating balanced meals. He has no appetite.

(6) *He finds himself more dependent on stimulants and/or sedatives.*

I'm not talking addiction, although dependency may be a problem. I'm talking about moving from one or two cups of coffee to eight, ten, and twelve cups of coffee because the energy level is not functioning as he wants it to function. More and more sugar is taken in. He has difficulty sleeping without a mild sedative. If the problem gets severe, he is making more trips to the physician to get some help to soothe his nerves and help him get to sleep at night.

(7) *He exercises when the urge hits, but it hits infrequently.*

The pattern of exercise is hard to get into. He finds more excuses not to exercise than he finds reasons to exercise.

After a vigorous exercising activity, he gets out of bed the next day so sore and uncomfortable that he can hardly move. The next day when it is time to get back into the working pattern, he remembers how he hurt the day before, and it discourages his enthusiasm. He does not exercise, until he begins to feel guilt for the extended area above his belt, then he tries it again. He becomes predictably irregular with his exercise.

(8) *He takes on fewer and fewer responsibilities.*

When the enthusiasm is not there, it is difficult to get excited about doing some of the things that previously were exciting.

Contrary to what many think, decreasing activities, for a person who has what some behaviorists call Type A behavior, does not increase fulfillment. The lack of activities increases burnout. Type A behavior is that behavior in people that causes them to want to take on many varied and difficult tasks because their energy level is high. These people enjoy doing things their way and find doing things their way gives them a great deal of satisfaction. A dramatic change to doing only a few of the things that previously were interesting can give the body a "rhythm shock." The drama involved in doing fewer things may cause the burnout which he so fears and dreads.

(9) *He places high value on making it on less rest.*

Our work ethic has done much to shape many of our best values. Our work ethic has also equated activity with production for many of us. The minister who was reared on this work ethic finds himself relying on the value of trying to make it with less rest than he needs. Then he finds himself tired at too frequent intervals. He has a twofold attitude toward what he feels about making it on less rest. He wants others to know that he is able to make his schedule on very little rest. But then he does not have the energy to keep his commitments, therefore he feels guilt that he is not able to follow through.

(10) *He begins to carry a constant comrade: exhaustion.*

He carries exhaustion to bed with him. He carries exhaustion to breakfast when he gets up. He carries exhaustion to the pulpit . . . ad infinitum.

This feeling is more severe than simply feeling tired (as we discussed earlier). This is exhaustion. He feels like nothing else but sitting, or sleeping.

(11) *He begins to live with full-time unavoidable vulnerability.*

When the minister faces burnout with the symptoms described above, he is vulnerable. He is spiritually distraught to the point of being more subject to the preying of the tempter than at any other time in his life.

Jesus' humanity is clearly seen in facing the tempter. His first test occurred in the wilderness. After forty days of fasting in the wilderness he was hungry. The tempter offered a shortcut. The tempter consciously offered the special lure of something for nothing. Jesus was vulnerable. That is what burnout does to us physically. Jesus' response was, "Man shall not live by bread alone, but by every word that proceedeth out of the mouth of God." He was ready with strength. Hopefully, the minister can be ready with strength. The bread may be in the form of envy because his brother in a church in the same association had twelve decisions on the previous Sunday. He had been fed with the bread of life. But the minister himself had no decisions. He was starving. He was vulnerable. He must remind himself that he will be fed. There are other ways that God's will can be done in ministry.

The tempter tried again while Jesus was vulnerable. He suggested that if Jesus wanted to make his mark, he must impress the people. He must give a visible, tangible, and dramatic demonstration. He should give a sign.

A friend of mine felt he was being squeezed into a resignation. A deacon came to him and suggested, "Why not let next Sunday be the test. If we have any decisions for Christ next Sunday morning, then God is telling us you are still the man for our church. If there are no decisions, then certainly you must agree that something is wrong. And, understand, Pastor, I will be praying for you that the sign does occur." My friend said he was immediately reminded of the situation with the tempter suggesting to Jesus that what he needed was a sign to establish his messianic authority. This time Jesus quoted from Deuteronomy: "It is written again, Thou shalt not tempt the Lord thy God." Correspondingly, my friend is still in the same church. The deacon is not. He went on to join a charismatic movement.

I recall hearing a pastor who served as a missionary for more than thirty years in China. I heard him preach at the Big Springs Baptist camp in Van Buren, Missouri in 1956. I remembered the poetic title of one of his sermons, "The Devil Will Get You While You're Down; Give God the Freedom to Pick You Up." To illustrate his sermon, he told a group of ministers, be careful with your spiritual and emotional life immediately following a great revival. Your defenses are down. You are most vulnerable after a spiritual experience. Jesus was in the conclusion of a great spiritual experience of fasting. The devil was trying to get him while he was down . . . or vulnerable. The minister is most likely to sin when he is vulnerable.

To continue with the analogy, the third test was the tempter's trump card. He was ready to play out his hand, as I heard Dr. Herschel Hobbs phrase the third temptation in a sermon. The tempter showed him all the kingdoms of the world. He was ready to give a little and take a little: compromise. All I want, he suggested, is that you fall down and worship me. Jesus was able to confront the temptations during his vulnerability. Hopefully, the resources we have gathered before possible burnout will carry us through our temptations. It is certain that we need God most when we are down and vulnerable. We must not compromise our convictions.

One other word about vulnerability. Being *up* may be to be *down*. In other words, when we are high on our own joys of accomplishment, we are likely to think too highly of our own skills. We may then be most vulnerable. We must then remember our Creator. We must then remember who we are about . . . what our mission is . . . what God has called us to do. The minister who had the decisions for Christ and is gloating to his colleagues may be just as vulnerable as the man who has had no decisions. He may be on an ego trip. The tempter can tempt him just as easily as he can the minister who had no decisions.

Perhaps it will give a more concise picture if we look at the danger signals all together. The danger signals of burnout in physical life of the minister are:

(1) He begins to feel tired frequently;
(2) He begins to gain weight;
(3) He spends fewer hours at previously favorite activities;
(4) His sexual energies have waned;
(5) He begins to lose weight;
(6) He finds himself more dependent on stimulants and/or sedatives;

(7) He exercises when the urge hits, but it hits infrequently;
(8) He takes on fewer and fewer responsibilities;
(9) He places high value on making it on less rest;
(10) He begins to carry a constant comrade: exhaustion;
(11) He begins to live with full-time unavoidable vulnerability;

Not all ministers have *all* the danger signals. One minister cannot gain weight and lose weight at the same time. Perhaps he has only two or three, but the symptoms are indicative of how some ministers respond physically to burnout in their lives.

Now what can be done about these Danger Signals?

A PRACTICAL GUIDE TO AVOID PHYSICAL BURNOUT

Certain sensible steps can be taken to cut off the burnout danger signals before they become immobilizing. (See Figure 3.)

A BALANCED BREAKFAST SHOULD INCLUDE

. . . eggs (no more or less than three or four a week
　　unless on a special diet)
. . . low-fat milk, or low-fat cheese
. . .whole grain or enriched breads and cereals
. . . fruit juice
. . . some additional kind of fruit
. . . lean meat, poultry, or fish

FIGURE 3

(1) *Eat right and sensibly.*

Dozens of studies have been done on stress and its resulting burnout during the early 1980s. One of the most frequently suggested ways to deal with burnout (physical burnout) is to eat right and sensibly.

This means a healthy breakfast. My early ministry was distraught with early morning rituals of rushing into the day without proper preparation. A cup of coffee would hold me until I had a chance to get a doughnut. I could not understand why I was having difficulty with my digestive system. Now I know. I was not eating a good breakfast.

A good balance of the foods mentioned above in Figure 3 will ensure that you get the nutrients necessary for high energy and low cholesterol.

Cornflower oil or margarine that contains vegetable oils should be taken with no more than two to three tablespoons daily.

Baked goods should be eaten sensibly. Sugar should always be refined. Sauces and whole milk products should be eaten only moderately. Candy and soft drinks should be virtually eliminated unless the sugar intake in your system is in an imbalance.

Not only will eating properly help the energy level, studies have proven that a healthy diet will help you build resistance to infection. This is particularly true during the winter months. Consult your physician for a diet to meet your own individual needs. He will also help you to know how overweight you are, and if necessary, what kind of diet will help you get back to your proper weight.

You can lose as much as one pound every twelve days if you cut only 300 calories a day from your present intake. A slow and safe program of losing weight is always the best because there is no metabolic shock to the system.

A vitamin and mineral supplement is available in every supermarket and drugstore. This will assure you of the appropriate amount of nutrients necessary for your body. It may also increase your appetite. You should be alerted to the fact that if your body is getting the appropriate amount of vitamins, minerals, and nutrients, it will be using more energy and thus have a healthier appetite. Be careful not to overreact to the new healthy attitude by eating even more.

(2) *Plan your relaxation and meditation periods.*

John F. Kennedy was said to be particularly fond of his "five minute vacations." He would take five minutes of each hour to relax. Often he would sit in his favorite rocking chair and close his eyes for an immediate release from the world around him. This is a good idea. I have tried it and wish I could form a habit of this "five minute vacation" concept.

There are a number of helps for relaxation responses to the body. Any bookstore is plentiful in resources for the autogenic planned relaxation exercises.

SOME RELAXATION EXERCISES

one—Isolate yourself from all noises. Get away from the phone. Get in a room where you cannot hear the voices of other persons. Pull the shades. Sit in a comfortable chair. Close your eyes. Make a deliberate effort to relax all your muscles. Start with your head. The very top of your head. Pretend that a heavy weight is being placed on the top of your head and is weighting your whole body down into the chair. Feel the weight go down the back of your neck. Let the concentration stop momentarily on the back of your neck. Relax all the muscles in the back of your neck and into the back part of your back. Allow yourself eight to ten minutes for this weight to take all the tenseness out of your entire body.

two—Again, sit in a comfortable position in a chair. Concentrate on your two arms. Let your arms fall completely down into a relaxed position. Concentrate on how heavy these arms have become. The left arm first. Then the right arm. Then do the same thing for your legs and feet. Concentrate on them one at a time. Cancel the exercises by opening your eyes and shifting your body and then repeat the process several times. Allow yourself about six to eight minutes for this exercise.

three—Lie flat on your back. Get into a room that is separate from noises. Be sure the place where you lie is not so soft that you lose the consciousness of the relaxation and simply want to go to sleep. Pretend warm water is being poured all over your body. Start at the top of your head and permit the water to be poured slowly (in your mind only) all up and down your body. Be sure the water is not too cold or too warm. It is just comfortable. Turn on your stomach and repeat the process. (The first time I tried this exercise I actually felt like I should get a towel and dry off. I hope you are as successful in your relaxation fantasy.)

four—By no means fourth in importance is the relaxation exercise brought on by reading the Scriptures and withdrawing into a prayerful attitude of replenishing the energies. Read two or three unfamiliar Psalms. Read those that are not already memorized. Read them softly but read them aloud. Close your eyes and envision what you think the psalmist was doing when he was writing the psalm. If he was sitting in a room behind a desk, pretend you are. You have become the psalmist. Then in your prayerful attitude ask God to give your body the needed replenishing nourishment necessary for the fatigue that you are feeling.

five—Read portions of devotional materials which will help you to get into a frame of mind separate from the disturbing influences around you. For example, do not try to read an entire book. Get several books that are easy to understand and easy to read but have profound devotional impact. You may wish to get unfamiliar material. Many are quite comfortable reading devotional material which is already familiar to them. Some examples are:

Thomas á Kempis, *Of the Imitation of Christ*, especially chapters 20 (Of the Love of Solitude and Silence), 1 (of second book) (Of the Inward Life); 5 (Of the Wonderful Effect of Divine Love); 7 (On Grace Kept Hidden for the Sake of Humility). These are but a few of the marvelous devotional thoughts of a seventeenth-century Christian.

Elizabeth O'Connor, *Search For Silence*. Especially the exercises following each chapter. Portions of devotional material are built into the book for easy reading and easy contemplation. For example,

"My children, mark me, I pray you. Know! God loves my soul so much that his very life and being depend upon his loving me whether he would or not. To stop God loving me would be to rob him of his God-hood."[1]

Reuel L. Howe, *Herein Is Love*. See especially pp. 82 ff., "Those Who Would Love," which deals with the power of the personal—God who is love. "The primary vocation of the Christian in this time is to respond to the call of the person to be personal. . . . The church is important, but it does not find its meaning in its isolation from the world. And knowledge about God, His creation, and redemption is necessary to the Christian life, but such knowledge must find its meaning in our living relation with God."[2] This is but one example of the beautiful devotional thinking of a man of God who has spent decades in helping other ministers find meaning in their own lives.

Hardy R. Denham, Jr., *Living Toward a Vision*. See especially chapter 5, "The Devotions of Life." In this chapter, Denham discusses the importance of understanding the biblical love for oneself, loving God as a part of the devotion of life, and the logical outcome of these two loves which is to love people. ["Owe no man any thing, but to love one another: for he that loveth another hath fulfilled the law" (Rom. 13:8).]

(3) *Plan a sensible exercise program.*

The key word in this phrase is "sensible." Working out feverishly for two or three weeks and then stopping the program is actually worse than having no program at all. The inconsistency keeps an imbalance in the metabolic system.

If you are planning a jogging program, be sure to start slowly. A plan for jogging is best suggested by a physician. If you are over forty, be sure to start with walking one or two miles per day. Work up to jogging. Jog every other day until you build up your system and wind. Your heart will respond best to the pressure of a regular program more than a rigid program.

If your schedule calls for an excessive amount of travel, learn to run in place for fifteen or twenty minutes per day. Some motels and hotels plan for joggers. Others do not. The area around some motels and hotels are often too dangerous for jogging at unusual hours.

It is with this urgency of preservation of the body that Paul admonishes the Romans, "Therefore, I urge you, brothers, in view of God's mercy, to offer yourselves as living sacrifices, holy and pleasing to God—which is your spiritual worship" (12:1, NIV). He is suggesting that we take care of our bodies.

Separate your work from your play. It is true that many people have been won to Christ on the golf course or on a tennis court. Christ should be shared wherever we are. It should be a natural part of our life to witness for Christ. But winning people to Christ is a part of what we are and a part of what we do. There is nothing wrong with wanting to play golf because it is fun. It will revitalize us and make us better soul-winners for Christ. If people are won to Christ as a by-product, it is wonderful. If the only reason we play golf is to try to win people to Christ, we are not playing for fun. At least, we are not playing for the exercise of the body. In my judgment, it is OK to do both—play for fun and win the lost, as well.

Plan an exercise program that you enjoy. Those who complain about jogging but continue to jog are not convincing when they say it is miserable. There is a payoff. There must be a payoff if the exercise program continues. Some pastors get their exercise by playing racquet ball or handball. These persons are close enough to an athletic club to have facilities. Many churches, in their program of activities, have provided facilities in their buildings. Many churches are seeing the value and the spiritual implications of good daily bodily exercise.

If golf is the only physical exercise outlet, be sure walking the course is a part of the schedule. Riding a golf cart does very little for the physical rejuvenation of the body. It may help emotionally. But it is limited in physical benefits.

(4) *Keep to a regular sleep schedule.*

Sleep is the program of renewal of the body. God planned it that way. To violate this program is to violate a part of the planned intention of the creative process. If possible, try to get your body conditioned to a regular program. If going to bed at 10:30 PM, following the news, is comfortable, then stick to it. Get up at 6:00 or 6:30, and begin your day refreshed. If this does not work, be sure your hours of sleep are consistent.

When I was in seminary, I usually went to bed at 1:00 or 1:30 AM. My body became accustomed to that schedule because of the study needs. I arose about 7:00 or 7:30. Now I find my body needs about one more hour of sleep to function best. It is important to know what your own body needs are in order to balance out your rest habits.

If your body needs help in going to sleep, see a physician. With all the convenient sleep and rest chemicals available, it is too easy to treat the symptom of sleeplessness and not the cause. If sleeplessness continues, get some feedback from a professional. The stress may be more deeply rooted than you have anticipated.

(5) *Discipline yourself to withdraw.*

One of the most disturbing phone calls a minister receives is, "Pastor, I know this is your day off, but. . . ." We have all been there. We are caring, compassionate persons with a desire to serve. How can we turn down a beginning like that?

Many ministers have found that it is impossible to withdraw for a day (take a day off) without withdrawing from the environment of living and working. Some have left town completely to spend time several miles away from their church fields.

The trap is in making a value judgment on being available seven days a week. I went to New Salem Baptist Church in Bardstown, Kentucky, in 1962 as pastor. One of the introductory remarks I made was, "I am always available when you need me . . . seven days a week." Mr. Beckham Cook, whom I grew to love for his wisdom, came to me after church service. In his whimsical manner, he said, "Parson, I would spend a lot of time thinking about that statement before you make it again. Lots of people will take you up on it." He was right! I should not have made the statement. The pastor needs his energy to be effective at maximum strength. He will need refueling if he is to avoid burning out.

He cannot burn the candle at both ends and expect endless light.

One technique is having others protect your day off. If your church has a secretary, the secretary can be coached in helping you to take calls which can be returned on the following day, unless there is an emergency. Of course, both of us know that most emergencies can be dealt with the next day in the office. Deaths and accidents are different. Anxieties which appear to church members to be emergencies often can be dealt with even *better* on the following day.

(6) *Establish a feedback system.*

The life and manner of the minister should be monitored by someone other than the minister himself. The very worst way of dealing with burnout is to bury it inside. The idea of pretending that feedback is not necessary is dangerous to the health of the minister.

The lack of a feedback system is not a sign of strength—contrary to what many believe. To many the idea of getting feedback is a sign of weakness. To others it is a sign that our spiritual lives are not in sync.

Someone should be consulted frequently about how the minister appears to be physically. To find someone is often difficult. It is, however, possible. The idea is to learn to trust someone to be honest enough with you to help you to know if you appear to be overly or dangerously tired. This person should help you to understand when you appear to be angry or withdrawn. Just as a physical examination tells the body what the status of health is, someone can help you know how you appear to the congregation.

To summarize the ways to deal with the physical symptoms of burnout, let us reflect on these mentioned,

(1) Eat right and sensibly;

(2) Plan your relaxation and meditation periods;

(3) Plan a sensible exercise program;

(4) Keep to a regular sleep schedule;

(5) Discipline yourself to withdraw.

(6) Establish a feedback system.

We are now ready to move on to one of the most dangerous ingredients of burnout: guilt.

5

Feeling Good About Feeling Bad — Irrational Guilt

There are at least two ways *to live under God's grace*.
1. To feel good about feeling bad—The result being self-imposed immunity from the joy of grace . . . *irrational guilt*.
2. To feel *good* about feeling good—The result being contagious optimism under Christ . . . *rational grace*.

Feeling down on oneself is seductive. It seduces us into believing that there is a payoff for being down on ourselves. The result is to begin to feel good about feeling bad.

Some boast about burnout. It is the "in" thing to talk about.

Recently a minister was talking to a dentist friend who was also a member of the church he served. The dentist was complaining about the high rate of suicides among dentists. "I suppose it is because no one really enjoys our company professionally!" said the dentist. He went on to say, "How would you like to spend all of your professional hours working with people who did not want to see you?"

The minister thought a moment. Then he said, "We have the same problem. No one really enjoys the company of a minister until they feel miserable. In fact, we probably spend most of our professional hours trying to make them feel miserable." Both men laughed. But as the minister was telling the story, I reflected on some of my own thoughts. Almost all humor has some element of truth in it. The miserable feeling we have and the miserable feeling we give people is magnetic. We are drawn to where pain is. We must work at being redemptive and working through the pain, both for ourselves and for others. We must not get stuck in enjoying the down side of ministry.

THE DOWN SIDE

Irrational guilt can be simply defined. It is the feeling that we are getting a raw deal and and we deserve it because of who and what we

72

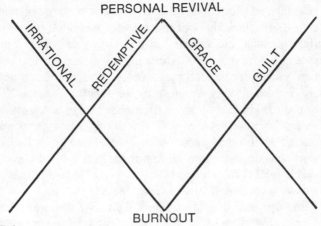

FIGURE 4

are. Obviously, that is an oversimplification. (See Figure 4.)

Rational guilt is deserved. We believe, "All have sinned, and fall short of the glory of God" (Rom. 3:23, ASV). We also believe redemptive grace resolves rational guilt. "For the wages of sin is death; but the free gift of God is eternal life in Christ Jesus our Lord" (Rom. 6:23, ASV). (See again Figure 4.) Again, "Nevertheless death reigned from Adam until Moses" (5:14a, ASV). In a word, we are all *guilty*.

But we are also under grace. Sin has been forgiven. Just as we believe Romans 3:23, Romans 6:23, and Romans 5:14, we also believe, "For if by the trespass of the one the many died, much more did the grace of God, and the gift by the grace of the one man, Jesus Christ, abound unto the many" (Rom. 5:15, ASV).

It is easier to be down on yourself than to be up on yourself. It is easier because other people accept it more easily. The Scriptures teach us to disapprove of sin. The minister is often seen as representing both God and the Scriptures. It follows in the minds of many that the minister should be "disapproving." Many begin to spend more time teaching the follies of sin than the foundation of grace. Being down on sin becomes a habitual behavior pattern. Many ministers can not separate the idea of being down on sin and being down on himself.

To complicate things for the minister and to assist him in his feelings of being down on himself, he adds shame. Feelings are a normal part of the humanity of each of us. Feelings such as anger, grief, pleasure, and fear are normal and should be anticipated for the purpose of being able to deal with them humanly. But the minister feels that he should not have certain feelings. He should not feel anger. He should even be careful about how he feels grief. Certainly he should be discriminating about when and where he feels pleasure . . . if at all. Fear is not in his vocabulary. He simply cannot afford to feel fear.

He was proud. He told his story dramatically. He was even excited about how he described his own reactions during the business meeting. He was respected and recognized by his peers. How he looked after he told his story was uppermost in his mind. He had wanted a minister of education. He felt his church was ready for one. He had presented it to the deacons with verve and energy. Two deacons, whom he felt did not support him, opposed the idea. They warned the pastor that they would object to the proposal on the floor of the business meeting even though the deacons had voted to approve the idea and present it to the church for consideration.

As the Wednesday neared, his anxiety level had been at a high peak. He had thought once about getting together with the two men for lunch to try and persuade them of their error. He had decided against it. He reasoned that they would be insulted. After all, he did not want to hear their side. He only wanted them to hear his side. He wanted them to be convinced that the church was ready for a minister of education.

The conversation went something like this. "The Personnel Committee, after consulting with the pastor, brings this recommendation to the church, that we call a minister of education. The details of hiring procedures and financial negotiations have been postponed until the church votes. The deacons have been consulted and have agreed that the church is ready for this major move. What is the church's pleasure?" The pastor had read the statement aloud, rather than the chairman of the personnel committee. He felt this would add more clout.

"I move that we adopt the recommendation," said one of the members of the personnel committee, who was also a deacon.

"I second the motion," said another.

"Any discussion?" the pastor asked.

The spokesman for the two deacons stood. "We want the best for our church just as all in this congregation do. We feel that it is not in the best interest of the church to make this decision at this time. Our reasons are pretty simple. We think the pastor got a little carried away when he attended a seminar on organizational procedures in a Baptist church. Some of the larger congregations and more influential people convinced him that our church was ready. We don't feel that these people know our church. We feel our pastor has been manipulated."

He sat down.

"Is there any other discussion," the pastor asked.

The second deacon spoke. "We would like to hear our pastor's reasons for thinking we are ready for a minister of education.

The second deacon sat down.

Long silence.

"Any other discussion?" asked the pastor.

The first deacon spoke again. "You mean you are not going to respond?"

Again, a long silence.

"It seems to me you owe us some kind of response."

"I am simply praying that God will have his way in the action of our church tonight."

The discussion ended abruptly.

The pastor won the battle. The vote was overwhelmingly in favor of calling a minister of education.

The pastor was proud of his ability to deal with the problem with very little discussion. In fact, it appeared he was even prouder of the fact that he had dealt with the problem with virtual silence. He felt he had shown no anger, even though he considered the attack against the proposal as an attack on him personally. He had shown the congregation, in his own estimate, that he was not afraid of disapproval and rejection. He did not consider his passive aggressive manner of disposing of the discussion as that of response in anger. He was "turning the other cheek."

When one of his friends had suggested that he had handled the problem with more anger than he had received from the two deacons, he was shocked. He had not felt that he had "put down" the two deacons. He had acted in a very "Christian" way. The church had supported him. That proved that he was right.

Of course he wondered why he had felt so "down" after the victory. He felt depressed for several days. Not long after that the two deacons and their families moved away from the church and joined an adjoining suburban church.

The down side of feeling bad had its compensations. He did feel that the church needed a minister of education. Nothing worthwhile comes easily. Some one had to make the sacrifice if the church was to be aggressive in moving into the future.

It was predictable that the minister would feel down after his victory. If a person will not allow himself the luxury of feelings such as anger, grief, pleasure, and fear, these feelings end up somewhere else. If unexpressed, they will be channeled. In this case, they were channeled into depression. The more serious the burial, the more serious the depression.

It is not abnormal to have feelings. "Feeling states, such as anger, grief, pleasure, fear, and all of the physical feelings, are a normal part of the humanity of each one of us. There is no such thing as an abnormal feeling state. . . . When you feel something, it is as much a normal part of you as the nose on your face or the hand on the end of your arm."[1]

If justification for feelings are important, consider the feelings of Jesus. "And he made a scourge of cords, and cast all out of the temple, both the sheep and the oxen; and he poured out the changers' money, and overthrew their tables" (John 2:15, ASV). Jesus was angry when he drove out the moneychangers from the Temple.

In Mark 3:5, we have an account of both anger and grief of Jesus: "And when he had looked round about on them with anger, being grieved at the hardening of their heart."

In Mark 14:36, he felt fear. "And he said, Abba, Father, all things are possible unto thee; remove this cup from me: howbeit not what I will, but what thou wilt" (ASV).

And in 1 Peter 2:23, he felt pain. "Who, when he was reviled, reviled not again; when he suffered, threatened not; but committed himself to him that judgeth righteously" (ASV).

If Jesus was afforded the luxury of human pain, fear, grief, and anger, then certainly, we who minister with less perfection, can admit to our own.

GUILT AND GRACE

Paul Warner describes two kinds of guilt in his book, *Feeling Good About Feeling Bad*. One kind of guilt is the rational kind. Guilt should follow sin. When the Christian breaks the moral law of God, he should feel guilty. He should deal with the guilt. This is rational guilt. This kind of guilt is an inducement to more ethical behavior. We need it. We must have it to conduct ourselves in a way that is befitting our calling. But the problem is with irrational guilt. Irrational guilt is the guilt that occurs for no apparent reason.

One of the chief causes of irrational guilt is the "ought" trips persons put on us. More correctly, it is the "ought" trips we "permit" persons to put on us. We do not have to choose these guilt trips. We permit them to occur because we develop some kind of obligation to these persons. It may be a deacon. It may be a wife or a child.

The temptation to commit adultery should quicken the conscience. Feelings of guilt should deter irresponsible behavior and sin. But when a deacon, wife, or child, feels their judgment of another behavior for him is more correct and encourages this behavior for him, the minister should be careful not to confuse morality with someone else's need to control his behavior.

A friend of mine shared this example. He was involved in a discussion about guilt and grace. Each person in the discussion was attempting to draw conclusions about the implications in their own lives. The friend, with obvious embarrassment, shared that he consistently felt guilty if he did not cook his wife's breakfast before he went to the church office. His wife did not work. She was at home all day and was healthy. She had lived in a tradition of congeniality in this arrangement between her own father and mother when she was growing up. She felt that a part of the chivalry of manhood was in showing some kindness to the lady. She measured the kindness by his willingness to cook her breakfast before he went to work. He resented the idea of doing it because it was expected of him. He had tried several times to break the habit of cooking breakfast for his wife. Each time he did not cook the breakfast he said he felt miserable all morning. He felt it was a better arrangement to cook breakfast in order to alleviate the feeling of guilt. He was caught in the jaws of a vise. He was a creature of captivity . . . the captivity of "shoulds" and "oughts." If he had chosen the gesture himself, he is convinced it would not bother him so much. He did not choose the behavior. He resented it. It is true that this problem should be negotiated between the two people involved. They should work out an agreed upon arrangement. It is also true that the guilt which he felt was irrational guilt. His wife had put a guilt trip on him. More correctly, he had allowed his wife to put a guilt trip on him. He could have refused this feeling of guilt. The difference between rational guilt and irrational guilt is that the fear of rational guilt is a legitimate deterrent of sin and irresponsible behavior. Irrational guilt is the result of permitting others to dictate behavior which otherwise you would not choose.

More must be considered about grace. If irrational guilt is a part of the operational behavior of the person, then he should have operative grace. Grace is the unmerited favor of God, it is true. But more mundanely, grace is the ability to live with one's own limitations. Grace can give the freedom to measure what is rational and what is irrational. Grace is the ability to deal with the expectations of others and still be free to choose your own behavior. That task is not simple . . . nor is it easy. To allow a wife the luxury of expectations without building resentment toward her because of it takes much grace. This must be the kind of grace that frees one to act and be without interference of the wants and needs which affect his or her own life.

Guilt is estrangement. We feel estrangement from God when we sin. We feel estrangement from others when we sin and the sin affects their lives. We feel estrangement whether the guilt is rational or irrational. Grace is more corrective of relationships. Grace is redemptive. Grace heals the estrangement which occurs between God and man. If one must grapple with guilt, both rational and irrational guilt, then he should have a workable concept of grace.

RECYCLING GUILT THROUGH RESPONSIBLE CONFLICT

What happens when we get down? The world loses its luster. The people with whom we relate are no longer the same compatible people we related to previously. We are seeing things through the buried feelings which have lured us into this martyrdom complex. But do we have to maintain this "poor pitiful pearl" attitude? Of course not. We believe in change. We think that grace can change even the most stubborn behaviors.

One way to reawaken grace is to recycle guilt. Turn the guilt into something constructive. It should be obvious by now that it is impossible to dismiss it from our person without God's help. We can, however, with God's help recycle the energy which guilt has thwarted. We should learn the redemptive force of conflict.

Conflict is not irresponsible attack. Conflict which is responsible is a way of caring for another person. When one has conflict with another, he or she feels intensely about that person. If the intense feelings are negative, then why not change these intense feelings into some positive feelings and ultimately, redemptive feelings.

As a way of legitimizing this possibility, consider the alternative. Apathy or not responding to conflict, can lead to resentment . . . or even worse, perpetual anger, better known as hate. Not participating in conflict when the feelings of anger have occurred is identified in psychological jargon as passive aggression. Many Christians who feel that they are turning the other cheek are in reality *turning on another burner. This burner cannot be seen. It is an oven.* And everyone knows that an oven generates much more heat than a burner. Not fighting, as the pastor chose to do in the business meeting in the company of the two deacons, is better identified as passive aggression. He is participating in the conflict, but he is not fighting fair. He is not showing his weapon. His weapon is more clandestine. He is urging the disapproval of the congregation by putting them down through his silence. He is not giving them the satisfaction of dignifying their opposition. He is "dehumanizing" them by making them feel they are fighting God and the church by disagreeing with the pastor. Although it is difficult to admit, it is possible that the two deacons could be right. The church just might not have been ready for a minister of education. I have a right to that opinion about the pastor because that pastor was me. I wish I could do it all again, but I'll try to learn something from that fiasco I pulled.

But how can conflict be a way of recycling guilt? It is possible. Grace must be administered, but it is possible. Warner suggests five rules for doing so. He suggests that conflict can be more than simply turning guilt into something constructive. He suggests that conflict can be fun. That might be pushing it a little far, but it is worth considering.

"Rule One: Each person speaks only for his own feelings.[2] Whenever someone else tries to express what he or she is feeling or say that he shouldn't be having that feeling, the other is in violation. They are out of bounds. They are hitting below the belt. The first rule of fighting fair and expressing feelings that will recycle guilt is to speak for yourself. No one should speak for you about feelings. This is another way of saying each person should withhold judgment, except on himself or herself.

"Rule Two: Anyone can say anything he wants to about his own feelings as long as he takes responsibility for the results.

"Rule Three: None has to say anything he does not want to say about his own feelings."[3] This frees the situation from unbridled candor. Unbridled candor can be devastating. In participating in conflict with care it is essential that the person find the right atmosphere for expressing his or her own feelings. Sometimes the atmosphere is not right for saying what one is feeling. It would be embarrassing or debasing. One does not have to say about their feelings what they do not choose to say. Kindness is always appropriate for the Christian.

This contributes to the respect of one for another. Giving the other person freedom to be silent is as essential as giving the other freedom to say what they feel about themselves. It enhances self-esteem. Being respected is important to those who have difficulty in feeling good about themselves.

"Rule Four: Absolutely no violence when expressing feelings."[4] Recently, a pastor friend of mine told me of an army sergeant who had felt the call to the ministry. He attended seminary at age thirty-four and began his ministry at age thirty-seven. During the first year, he twice challenged the pastor and associate pastor to settle their differences by "stepping outside." After actually shoving the pastor into the wall of his office, the deacons dismissed him. The former sergeant was mystified. "What is so bad about expressing anger with fighting?" he asked. When the deacons and the pastor explained to him that this kind of behavior was not only unacceptable, it was also unchristian, he still did not understand. He saw no problem with solving some problems with violence. This kind of thinking is simply unacceptable. Violence can not be allowed as a way of resolving conflict. The violation of the body is a violation of self-esteem. The damage is almost always irreparable. The sergeant needed much more than forgiveness. He needed some therapy which would help him to have respect for humankind.

A young man, age twenty-seven, was separated from his wife for the second time. The first time he had beaten her badly. The second time she left him and filed for divorce. He came to me for counseling. After two or three sessions he became comfortable enough to share some of the feelings that led him to punish her by beating her. He had hidden her glasses from her in order to stop her from leaving. She could not see without them. In the process, he had slapped one of the children across the face. He was a pathetic man who was trying to get the sympathy of the church. He came to each service and sat on the front row. He rededicated his life frequently. After each service, he had asked to talk with me. The feelings that he had become comfortable enough to share were that he felt that he should get back with his wife immediately, but that she must make some changes in her life. She must cook his evening meal. She had a job that demanded ten hours per day. She must spend more time cleaning. The house, he said, was always filthy. I want back with her, he said, but she must make some changes immediately.

I recommended that he see a therapist. I told him that I would not work with him until he agreed to get some help from the mental health center in the city where I was interim pastor. Why? he asked. Because you need to understand why you build up this rage and then explode, I told him. You need some help to understand that you must carry the responsibility for this kind of unacceptable behavior. You will not be good for your family until you learn to deal with the problem of uncontrolled rage in your life. I am happy to report that he got into a therapy program and the last communication I had was making progress in accepting the responsibility for his behavior.

He not only did not know how to recycle his guilt, he was not willing to accept the responsibility for his guilt. He tried to place the blame for his rage on someone other than himself. It is impossible to recycle guilt through some healthy manner of communication until the guilt is owned. It can not be blamed on someone else.

"Rule Five: Honesty when reporting feelings."[5] Jesus was honest enought to report his feelings. Each of us must also be honest. Honesty implies respect. The person owning the feelings shows respect for those who observe his feelings. Also the person owning the feelings shows respect for himself. Self-respect is an absolute must for those who wish to recycle guilt into a gracelike behavior.

Anger is another form of caring. If we do not care about persons enough to get angry with them, then we are certain to avoid them. But if we care enough about persons with whom we get angry, then we should care enough to work through the anger to a redemptive relationship.

Respect is an important ingredient for those who use conflict as a means of restoring relationships. Respect is another form of the Golden Rule. Warner suggested that the Golden Rule be interpreted, "The best way to keep from stepping on other people's toes is to put yourself in their shoes.[6] Second Timothy 2:24 teaches us, "God's people must not be quarrelsome; they must be gentle, patient teachers of those who are wrong" (TLB). With the appropriate gentleness and patience, respect is not far behind. Anger must never be expressed unless there is respect for the person in whose presence the anger is expressed.

"NOBODY APPRECIATES ME"

One of the resultant feelings of being down is that the minister begins to feel he is unappreciated. He waits for the affirmation which he felt he once got and he feels that it does not come.

Soon he is feeling that "they are doing this to me." It is too painful to carry the load of responsibility. He must blame someone. It must be them that is causing him to feel so miserable.

One pastor said, "I would not have come here had I known then what I know now. The pulpit committee was not honest with me. They did not tell me the whole truth."

"What could they have done differently?" I asked him.

"For one thing, they could have told me that I would not get the support I needed to get the program I wanted adopted."

"How did they know that then?"

"They could have told me what had gone on in the past in this church," he replied.

Another seductive feeling is that nobody appreciates us. The flow of conversation can become one of "Look at me! Do you not think that I am the most miserable of men? Why should I be the only minister to put up with this nonappreciative church? I am the most reviled of men." Feeling sorry for oneself is another way of getting needed attention. The minister who does not have adequate support systems finds himself looking for support in places where he cannot find it. He gets more removed. He finds himself more detached. He finds himself complaining more. He also finds a kind of distorted peace in asking for the sympathy from others that he cannot find in his church.

STEPS TO TAKE WHEN YOU'RE FEELING DOWN

It is not simple. It is not easy. Pulling oneself up by one's own bootstraps is difficult. But there are some practical steps that the minister can take in helping himself out of the doldrums. He can do something about his down side to get himself up. But he must take some deliberate actions. He must find a strategy. The following steps can be taken to begin the slow process of getting back up when you are feeling down and enjoying the down more than you should.

(1) First you must get in touch with your real feelings.

You cannot afford the luxury of losing your perspective. You must not rationalize that you are the only Christian left in your church, and thus it is inevitable that you feel down. To do this, you must take stock. You must look at your own anger when you are angry. You must look at your own fear when you are scared. You must look at your own pain when you are in pain. You must also find your source of joy and pleasure in order to find out what makes you come alive.

For that minister who stood so defiantly and martyr-like before his church in the presence of the two deacons (me, remember!) he could have begun with some nitty-gritties. He could have admitted that there was a possibility, even though remote, that he could be wrong. Perhaps the church is not ready for a minister of education. At least two members of the church were not ready for the minister of education.

Then he could have responded to their questions as they asked them rather than putting them down by the apparent "holier than thou" attitude that these men picked up from his silence. He could have been straight with them and talked with them about their side of the issue. In short, he could have admitted his own feelings and looked at his anger as the result of their not appreciating him as he thought they should. That approach is certainly not pleasant. It may, however, be redemptive.

(2) *With God's grace you can act yourself out of your own misery.*

God has given us the faculty of reasoning. He has also given us the feeling of being loved. With those two ingredients, you can act yourself out of your own misery.

Misery usually results from wanting something badly and feeling disappointed and irritated when you do not get it. In the case of the minister who wanted a minister of education, he had felt that his effectiveness as a minister depended on whether or not the church adopted his proposal. He was disappointed that not all the persons in the church wanted it as badly as he wanted it. He was irritated that he was being stymied in his efforts.

He was not aware of how demanding and insistent he was in the business meeting. He was not being cruel, but he was setting himself up for some misery if he did not get what he wanted.

Albert Ellis and Robert A. Harper wrote an interesting book, *A New Guide to Rational Living*, in which they suggest some practical ways of dealing with one's own sense of misery. "We distinguish, in consequence, between healthy feelings of sorrow or irritation when you lose something you clearly desire; and unhealthy feelings of depression or rage stemming from your childish refusal to accept a world with frustrations and losses, and from your whining that such things absolutely must not exist. If you choose to stay with these former feelings, you will feel appropriately disappointed or sorrowed at the loss of a person or thing you care for."[7]

To double the difficulty, when one does succeed in getting what one wants to relieve the misery, expectations become greater. Learning to live through the misery is the important ingredient for a redemptive life. Getting one's own way time after time builds a pattern. It becomes expected. But if miserable events occur and the misery is diminished by the presence of God and his grace, the living pattern becomes more tolerable. "You rarely ever completely win the battle against sustained psychological pain. When you feel unhappy because of some silly idea and you analyze and eradicate this idea, it rarely stays away forever, but often recurs from time to time. So you have to keep reanalyzing and subduing repeatedly."[8]

The story is told of Gaines Dobbins, a renowned Southern Baptist educator, sharing with a seminary class that no pastor would ever be worth his salt until a church had broken his heart. He was saying that misery can be a teacher. You can act yourself out of your misery and learn from it. Or you can bury yourself in it and live a life of misery . . . while complaining to those who will listen that the whole world has treated you wrongly.

(3) *You must prepare to be uncomfortable.*

God's grace is not an aspirin tablet for a temporary headache. God's grace is long lasting. It is often as therapeutic as an operation. An operation, as we all know, can be very painful.

The hidden payoff in being down is that we become comfortable with it. We understand being miserable. We have lived with it, and we know what to expect. But to do something about it, we must do something with which we are not comfortable. We may be very uncomfortable.

We may have to change our habits. We may have to change our way of doing the things that we have done in the same way for years.

(4) *Accept yourself as unique.*

No one else is like you. You are unique. That uniqueness can be a kind of excellence which is always growing in you. At some time in your life this quality or qualities of excellence have been demonstrated. Search out those times and concentrate on demonstrating them again.

God had something specific in mind when he created each of us. Our task is to find what that something specific is and build on it.

It will be much simpler to study the skills we have and dismiss them as ordinary. We can concern ourselves with the patterns of behavior which make us similar to others. Or we can study those patterns of behavior which make us know that we are individually unique.

(5) *Be a novice.*

Start again. Learn again. Be a novice.

The person who is self-energizing is the learner. The "down" person does not have time to learn. These people have learned what is necessary to get by and are satisfied just getting by. But the novice is one who grows. He or she does not have time to sit idly by and get bored with the skills already acquired. Being a novice is fun. It could be that there are many things about the work you are in now that you do not know. There are people in your church who have not shared who they are with you. Get to know them. Learn about their habits. Be a novice!

(6) *Listen for the melodies.*

The words are easy to pick up in communication. You can define and decipher words. But listening for the melodies of life takes a special kind of listening ear. The person who listens for the melodies listens for the moods and temperaments behind the words. The melody will build congruence. For example, if a minister says, "God loves you," but he does it with a scowl, the melody is incongrous with the words. There is something more going on. To listen for the melody is to find out what that something more is.

A small boy was riding home with his parents from church. "What was he mad about?" the boy asked.

"He was not mad, sweetheart! He was preaching on the love of God. He was showing how people could acquire the love of God by trusting him."

"But he yelled at us like he was mad at us," continued the boy.

"No, he was just excited about his message," replied the mother.

"He sure did sound a lot like Daddy when he gets mad at us," was the response.

The words and the melody did not come together as the little boy thought they should. Many of us communicate one thing with the words and quite another with the melody. The exciting part of life is to listen for those melodies. How can anyone afford the luxury of boredom when there are so many double messages being given by those around us. The alternative is to be oblivious to the more sensitive part of life. Often the most intense and revealing messages are those which are not phrased in words but suggested by intonations, inflections, and expressions.

CONCLUSION

Feeling good about feeling bad is tempting. Depression is easy. Getting up from the "downs" is difficult. When the fire is low and the rocking chair is comfortable, the minister has a choice. He can be lulled into the delusion that the fire will continue without wood. Or he can restoke the fire with the practical steps of dealing with irrational guilt with the grace of God. The fire will burn again . . . and brightly.

6

Burnout Is Anger Turned Inward

To be angry and sin is a wish to destroy a relationship. The biblical teaching to be angry and sin not is best described as a search for healing in a relationship.

What happens to the anger when it is kindled and has no place to go? What does the minister do with the hostile feelings which are as natural as breathing?

In the previous chapter we discussed the unhandled or mishandled guilt turned inward. We spoke of grace as one of the most important ingredients for the minister in dealing with guilt. What about the anger turned inward or downward and the result? It becomes *depression*. One reason burnout is such an insurmountable problem with many is that most do not know what to do with depression. Many will not admit that they have it to begin with, and then those who do admit it find it difficult to deal with.

In the previous chapter we also discussed the ways that healthy conflict (owning your own anger and dealing with it responsibly) is one way of dealing with guilt. Conflict, contrary to what many believe, is not merely the result of anger. Conflict, as was considered earlier, is a way of dealing with guilt.

DENIAL

One way of not feeling anger is to deny it. As a minister gets into the age of the forties and fifties he begins to feel less energy. He may even feel that pulpit and pastor selection committees are passing him by while they came frequently at an earlier age. He has two choices. He can face the fact that he is not as young as he used to be and adjust to the changes. Or he can deny that he is getting older and pretend he is the same person he was when he was in his early thirties. The advantages of being older are legion. The body, however, has made some significant changes. The energy level has begun to change. The perception of others of his age is different. Some younger people consider persons in their forties and fifties to be old. Those who are in their forties and fifties consider themselves to be young. Being conscious of the perception of others is just as important as being conscious of one self-perception. To deny that there have been changes is folly . . . and dangerous.

Many of the fears which cause denial of age are justified. Our society reflects the values of youth. Corporations replace older executives. Many churches begin to hope for the retirement of the minister who has gotten into his sixties. If he is not performing up to their expectations, he may find more than disapproval. He may find some moves to get him to retire. But to live with denial of age is dangerous. The danger is in the fact that the body must have adaptable resources. The shape of the body has changed. It is much easier to get out of shape when you begin to see forty and forty-five. It is harder to stay in shape. It is so easy to develop the bulging waistlines that characterize too many of our ministers. Denial causes many of these who suffer with bulging waistlines to be blind to their own infirmity.

Ministers who deny their age are likely to be those who deny their own anger. The two are corollaries. It becomes harder to embrace innovations and new methods. Putting down the changes is easier. Adusting is more difficult.

SYMPTOMS OF DENIAL OF ANGER (See Figure 5)

   (1) Exhaustion

Denial carries with it weariness. Not far behind is exhaustion. Exhaustion is hard to face. For the minister it is a complete reversal from the high energy level he grew accustomed to in his earlier ministry. He cannot keep on keeping on as he once did. He finds himself more in need of a nap to rekindle his energy. But then he feels guilty for taking a nap. He complicates his problem.

Exhaustion is nothing to be ashamed of. Instead, it is the body telling us what we need to know. The body is eager to keep the chemical processes in balance. It speaks to us with needs. If we listen to those

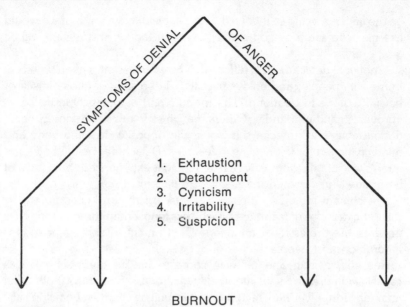

1. Exhaustion
2. Detachment
3. Cynicism
4. Irritability
5. Suspicion

BURNOUT

FIGURE 5

needs, we will learn to live with the way our system functions.

Exhaustion is the feeling of being dragged out. We feel as if we have been flattened by a steam roller and have no energy to lift ourselves. Rest is the healer. Find the spot. Lift the obligations to the point of releasing yourself from the denial that you need it and simply rest. Sleep. Sit Down. Do what is necessary to relieve the exhaustion.

(2) Detachment

Detachment is a more difficult device to deal with. Detachment is a self-protective device to ward off pain. Detachment will help avoid being rejected.

Detachment can be defined as separation. It may be physical separation. Or it may be emotional separation. The difference may be according to the individual. If it is physical separation, the minister will find someplace where he or she can be alone. This detachment can be healing. It can be the beginning of working through the anger. It is important to know that detachment is a way of dealing with anger. It may be the anger of not being able to accomplish all that we like. It may be the anger of being so involved with people that we feel as if we would like never to see a person again . . . even though this feeling will be temporary.

Emotional detachment is different. The effervescent person who is at home with people, and enjoys people, all of a sudden finds himself or herself wishing to be alone. The friendly and outgoing type becomes introvertish and unfriendly. Others may interpret this behavior as being discourteous and unfeeling. It is just the opposite. It is the body and mind crying out for the healing it deserves. Detachment is the body and mind's way of refueling. Any person who has experienced some form of burnout will understand the need for detachment.

Detachment must be monitored. Detachment can become dangerous. The need for detachment which lasts longer than three or four days needs some professional attention. Detachment in shorter periods is natural for most people.

Recently, a man and his wife came to me for counseling. I was especially impressed with the intelligence and sensitivity of both. The man, age forty-five, had been a minister until he changed vocations just three years earlier. He had gone into a local industrial firm. He came as a referral. He was depressed. He felt the need for some redirection. He felt more and more detached. It had started with the need for detachment from his church. He was a member of a strong church and had become an active member. Lately, however, he had dropped out of the activities of the church. He had been an outgoing person. Now he was withdrawn and detached. He had felt rejected from an important person in his life. It had affected all his other relationships. As he began to bury himself in his detachment, he became strangely anesthetized to his responsibilities to his family and friends. He had closed off the world. He had grown more and more into himself. He was so detached that he did not want to be around people. He became ill. All my efforts to help were thwarted. I felt helpless. I encouraged him to find some new interests and to take stock in what he already had going for him. I could not reach him. He had become so detached that he was unreachable. We prayed together. We talked together. We covenanted together to search out all the alternatives to his depression. I still could not reach him. He could not return to the real world. Although the problems were much more complex and disturbing than simple detachment, I have often wondered what would have happened if he could have found some direction before he became detached. He was angry. He took his anger out on himself. Whether or not his anger was justified is not the issue. He denied the anger toward others and took it out on himself.

Detachment should be dealt with before it becomes dangerous.

(3) Cynicism

The Bible speaks of the dangers of anger. "But if ye have bitter jealousy and faction in your heart, glory not and lie not against the truth. This wisdom is not a wisdom that cometh down from above, but is earthly, sensual, devilish. For where jealousy and faction are, there is confusion and every vile deed" (Jas. 3:14-16, ASV). The anger toward another turns into jealousy and faction in the heart. Anger results when one does not do or become what another would have that person do or become. We want what we think they have. They get it and deprive us of having what we think is rightfully ours. The result is cynicism.

Cynicism becomes the child of anger or jealousy of another. A minister lives in a world of production. He does what he feels is right in the sight of God. He serves in a manner for which he is proud. He serves "faithfully." His rewards, however, do not come as quickly as he wished. Often, he wants a larger church. He sees his friends being called to churches that he feels he could pastor. His competence is equal to, if not surpassing, theirs. He tries to remain humble. He prays that he will feel contentment in doing what he feels is God's will. But the malcontent feelings persist. He sees another of his friends called to a church that looked interesting. This friend was much younger than he. He is angry. Why are some more blessed than I? Am I not serving in a dedicated fashion? Yet I am not the one with whom the pulpit selection committees come to talk.

Soon he finds himself going to Monday morning minister's meetings and listening with a new and strange ear. Where before he could rejoice with those who shared their attendance and decision records, now he finds himself being a little more amused toward those who are successful in raising their records. He starts innocently enough. "Did you break another record yesterday, Jim, or was this one of those weeks when you were human like the rest of us?" He laughs nervously, but he finds Jim not too amused. Then a strange phenomenon occurs:

a new sensation which is foreign to his ordinary feelings. Before Jim answers, he finds himself hoping Jim "did not" break any records. He hopes Jim did not have as many decisions as he. He realizes how unchristian this feels to him, and thus begins to deny the feelings immediately. He may even try to cover his tracks. He may try to make amends. "I rejoice with your Sunday School attendance!" he says in a more serious vein. But the damage is done. He knows that there is an element of truth in his very first statement and he also knows that Jim knows that there is an element of truth in it.

(4) Irritability

Closely accompanying his newfound cynicism is his irritability. Patience had been one of his long suits. He had prided himself on his ability to remain calm through the heaviest of storms. His anger, unchanneled, has left him now in a different mind-set. He is irritable with those people with whom he has very little reason to be irritable.

He finds himself divided against himself. James described those feelings when he wrote, ". . . out of the same mouth cometh forth blessing and cursing, My brethren, these things ought not so to be. Doth the fountain send forth from the same opening sweet water and bitter? Can a fig tree, my brethren, yield olives, or a vine, figs? Neither can salt water yield sweet" (Jas. 3:10-12, ASV).

Facing his irritability, he reaches for the promises which follow a little later in the teachings of James in James 3:17-18, "But the wisdom that is from above is first pure, then peaceable, gentle, easy to be entreated, full of mercy and good fruits, without variance, without hypocrisy. And fruit of righteousness is sown in peace for them that make peace" (ASV).

He wants to be the one to sow peace, but his buried anger has left an unpleasant irritability which takes him by surprise, and takes those with whom he relates by surprise.

(5) Suspicion

When a compliment is paid, the frustrated minister becomes suspicious. "Wonder what he meant by that?" he laments when he is affirmed about his sermon. "What does he want from me?" he continues

Perspective is difficult. Before, he could see things in the broad context. Now he is seeing things in more tunnel-vision fashion. He sees only a small part of the total picture. He feels more "on trial" than before. He does not feel totally comfortable with the thank you's and "I appreciate you's."

It is only a small step from feeling unappreciated and suspicious to feeling mistreated. When things get this wrong, we definitely need some feedback and help from those who are significant to us and from those whom we trust. Clinically, it is called "paranoia" but the feeling is painful no matter what the label. It is best to deal with the feelings of suspicion before they become exaggerated. It is best to deal with suspicion before it becomes paranoia.

The draining effect of being suspicious is that it causes us to be on the alert and on the defensive. Spontaneity is the release necessary for uptightness, but the suspicious person uses all his energy protecting himself. There are no times for laughing, crying, playing, or simply enjoying. The release is not there to relieve the anxiety.

Additionally, the suspicious person has no trouble fighting back when he feels he is attacked. The suspicious person does not feel like he "starts" anything, therefore it is OK for him to fight back without feeling any guilt. His anger is not controlled anger any longer. He feels it's OK to turn loose unbridled candor and lash out even when the circumstances do not seem to warrant it. Suspicion has caused many ministers to get in deep water with authority figures in the church before they know what has happened to them. Then the result is that the suspicious person feels quite justified in fighting back with excessive energy because the authority figures were out to get him in the first place. Not long after, some of these ministers begin to communicate with their friends that their ministry is "not effective" in the church where they are presently ministering.

There is one other important aspect of suspicion to be considered. Suspicion is a self-fulfilling prophecy. In other words, when the suspicious person entertains more than an episode of suspicion and becomes suspicious toward others in almost all their dealings, people tend to shun them. Very few want to be with a person who does not trust them. The aura becomes believable. The suspicious person breathes suspicion so strongly that the aura says back to others, "You are not someone I trust, therefore, you must not be a trustworthy person." Friends get farther and farther away from them.

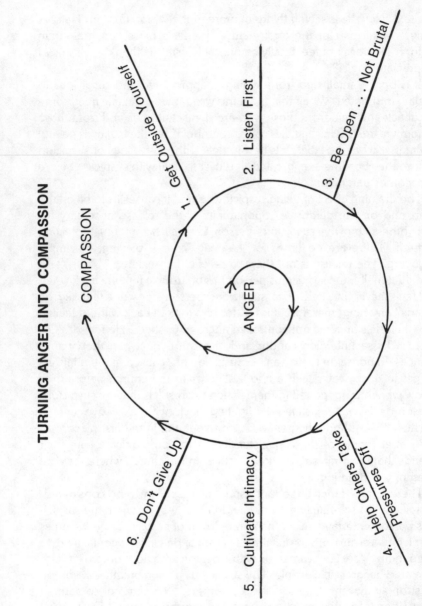

TURNING ANGER INTO COMPASSION

COMPASSION

ANGER

1. Get Outside Yourself

2. Listen First

3. Be Open . . . Not Brutal

4. Help Others Take Pressures Off

5. Cultivate Intimacy

6. Don't Give Up

FIGURE 6

ANGER IS DISTORTED LOVE

The same energy which is used to turn anger in on ourselves, can be used to love others as well as ourselves. The feelings of anger which turn to depression are powerful feelings. These feelings can be used productively by the minister. He cannot use them if he denies them. He cannot use them if he distorts them. He can use these feelings if he learns the practical ways of turning his own energy into the loving compassion God intended for them to be.

HOW TO TURN ANGER INTO COMPASSION

Both anger and compassion come from passion. The feelings of intensity can be channeled redemptively. How?

(1) Get outside yourself.

The first step in turning anger into compassion is to turn the feelings which lead to depression into the capable hands of God. Trust God to be able to deal with them. After reading that statement aloud, I realize how presumptuous it sounds. Some strong and capable minister is saying, "How dare he suggest that I have not been doing that!" That strong and capable minister has a legitimate basis for that statement. It is easy to get caught up in the secular humanistic movement and try to pull ourselves out of the depression by our own bootstraps. It is OK to try. But God can succeed where we will blunder. We must get outside our own omnipotent feelings of being able to handle all our problems and trust the healing power of God. We depend on the ultimate direction and healing that God can give us. We must persevere.

In the April 1981, issue of *Psychology Today*, Daniel Yankelovich wrote, in an article, "A World Turned Upside Down," that the self-fulfillment movement was giving way to a new society. The new society is more concerned for others than the society of the 1960's and the 1970's. He wrote, "In 1973, the 'Search for Community' social trend, whose status my firm measures each year, stood at 32 percent, meaning that roughly one-third of Americans felt an intense need to compensate for the impersonal and threatening aspects of modern life by seeking mutual identification with others based on close ethnic ties or ties of shared interests, needs, background, age or values. By the beginning of the 1980's, the number of Americans deeply involved in the Search for Community had increased from 32 percent to 47 percent. A large and significant jump in a few short years.[1] That is encouraging. The 'get inside yourself' movement is giving way to the 'get outside yourself' movement. The secular humanism of the 1970's is giving way to the Commitment personalism of the 1980's. That is a movement which may be entirely world-view and not simply Christian-view. If this is true, then the Christian has cause to rejoice. The Christian who is willing to get outside himself will find more solutions than problems."

Yankelovich continues, "Statistics such as these, taken together with other data, indicate the beginnings of a counter-trend away from a duty-to-self outlook."[2] The trend is one of hope and encouragement. If the Christian can get outside himself, he will find new ways to cope with the anger turned inward. He will find more freedom to have compassion as is taught in the Sermon on the Mount. The research findings show that the me-first, satisfy-all-my-desires attitude leads to superficial, transitory, and unsatisfactory relationships. The Golden Rule stands . . . beckoning us to life and hope.

(2) Listen first.

That is the entire statement. . . . Listen first. One of the major reasons that anger is unloosed into disaster is that most of us have not learned to listen. The listening is not only scriptural ["Ye know this, my beloved brethren. But let every man be swift to hear, slow to speak, slow to wrath" (Jas. 1:19, ASV)], it is affirming. It is affirming to those who speak in that you give them respect. It is affirming in learning because information is coming in and not simply going out.

Listen to your own needs in order to be free to listen to the needs of others. Listen to the heartbeat of your own wants and desires and measure them with your needs. In that manner, you will be free to listen to the needs of other persons. God does not expect us to have answers to all problems, but he does expect us to be willing to search for the answers to others' problems. To do that, we must listen.

There was a period in our history at the Baptist Sunday School Board, when we gave a battery of tests to discover the ability of persons to manage. One of the instruments measured *verbal ascendancy*. Now, in its more simple form, verbal ascendancy is simply the need to talk. But in its more complex form, it is the desire to control the agenda.

Ministers, you would expect, have higher than average verbal ascendancy. For a brief period, we averaged the verbal ascendancy findings. For that period, several months, we found that the verbal ascendancy of ministers averaged about 91 percent. That means that the persons who took the instruments were satisfied with the agenda if they were in control for 91 percent of the time. That leaves very little time for listening. If we need to control the agenda for 91 percent of the time, we would allow only 9 percent of the time to be given to others, and in that time, we must allow for our own boredom and fatigue from controlling the agenda. Not a very bright picture, but instruments are often wrong. Before getting too despondent, why not simply learn the better techniques for listening, and with that consciousness, lessen the need to control the agenda.

Important to good listening is remembering. Remember what has already been said. The subject matter can be a web of interesting data which will build when remembered. In a gentle, nonthreatening, and open-minded manner raise questions which will help the person to reason through his or her own problems. When others can feel that they have solved their own problems, they are usually grateful to those who have helped them. Remember what they have been saying in order to assist them to do just that.

Listening allows others to be a part of the plot. Talking or controlling the conversation causes others to feel that they are not a part of the plot. Somehow they seem less important when someone else is doing the talking. They also seem more important when they are doing a significant amount of the talking.

(3) Be open . . . not brutal.

Some are comfortable in being open. Others have to force themselves to be so. Some are brutal in their openness. It is what they call being honest.

I had done a rather poor job. I felt my preaching was subpar. My sermon did not have the crispness that I usually feel that it does. I was standing at the back of the congregation greeting the members of the church where I was interim pastor. She said, "That tie just does not go with that suit, Pastor." She smiled and waited for me to respond. I did not respond. She went on. "I don't mean anything by it. I just try to be honest with people, and I really think you could have made a better choice." She laughed nervously and went on out. I continued shaking hands with the members.

To say it did not set well with me would be an understatement. It made me angry. In the first place, I did not ask her. More importantly, she was right. On the other hand, I did not want to hear it that morning especially.

I had a history with her and that complicated the offhand remark. She had been robbed while she was in the hospital. She was fortunate enough to catch the thieves. One of the thieves was a thirty-two year-old woman who had a poor reputation in the community. Before the robbery, we had won the thief's sister to the Lord. I was waiting to baptize her when the robbery occurred. The possessions were recovered. We had several long conversations about the charges. The second thief was a sixteen-year-old boy. The court suggested that the thirty-two-year-old thief get psychiatric help. She did. She also began to counsel with me at the suggestion of the psychiatrist whom I knew.

Both the psychiatrist and I felt she was suicidal. She had tried to raise two children by herself. She was desperate for finances. She had tried to maintain a home for the children. She had made a number of mistakes in the community which caused her to be thought of in a light unbecoming any normal human being. This was her first offense.

After several weeks of painful counseling, the lady had called me to ask my opinion about the thief. I told her I thought the thief was suicidal. I suggested that she consider dropping the charges because I felt she was repentant. I also felt she had made a decision for Christ. The lady agreed that she would do it. She called the thief's sister and told her what she was going to do, but she did not. Week's passed and no move was made to drop the charges. I carried a lot of my own prejudices about her, thinking that she must be a little vindictive. However, I knew how she felt, having been robbed myself, later to drop the charges.

All of that history went behind the remark, "I don't mean anything by it. I just try to be honest with people." Had I not known her I would probably have received the statement much easier. But, on the other hand, the persons with whom we are open are usually carrying some kind of history in our relationship that will affect the statement.

We are discussing turning anger into compassion. Openness is essential to this deliberate strategy. To avoid building resentful attitudes, openness can help. But the tempering of openness is a must. The brutality of openness which comes out as unbridled candor to those who are supersensitive rarely builds compassionate feelings.

(4) Help others take the pressure off.

I have found that helping others take the pressure off of themselves takes the pressure off of me. I find myself listening more for my sake when I say, "Who says you have to do all that to be Christian!"

Most of us get lost in our feelings of guilt. We are not too sure that we have the ingredients of grace. We build a great case for grace. We talk about its permanence. But then we remember that we, too, are sinners. We know that we have done some pretty sinful things in our own lives. We are mad at ourselves for those sins. We don't want to carry the pressure of those sins with us. We look for the releases. In my judgment, if you can help others take the pressure off themselves, you can do some of the releases *for* yourself.

Some of the closest friends I have today are those with whom I have looked ridiculous and they have witnessed it. Sometimes they have been the recipients of my ridiculous acts. Once the pressure has been lifted, I have felt closer to them. I have found myself more caring about them than about those people who have been at arm's length emotionally.

(5) Cultivate intimacy.

Volumes have been written on intimacy. What is it? Who is entitled to it? When is it appropriate? Even more could still be written because intimacy is nothing more than getting close to others. How can one care for another if they are not intimate? Intimacy is being close enough to another to trust another person. Intimacy is being close enough to share the most humiliating moment in your life. Intimacy is the way one builds a bridge toward witnessing to another.

Perhaps the biggest barrier to intimacy is that we are afraid we will lose control of our self-esteem. We wonder, if others really knew us as we are would they still care? The answer is not uncomplicated. But most people who are Christians feel even more caring and close to people who know us as we are.

(6) Don't give up.

I must make a special effort to communicate again with the lady who insulted my tie. I must not give up. I was offended because of a lot of other garbage. But I know that the problem was not hers. The problem was mine. I want to own the fact that I was ready to be offended. God's grace can do that for me even if I don't want it to.

If anger is to be channeled into compassion, it must have time. We can not give up before the battle is won.

Most of us find times that we would rather quit. Moses did. Elijah did. Jeremiah did. It may be because of continual disappointment. It may be simply because we are tired. But we must not quit. I like the rhyming narrative of the following, because it expresses that mandate so beautifully:

> When things go wrong as they sometimes will,
> When the road you're trudging seems all uphill,
> When the funds are low and the debts are high,
> And you want to smile, but you have to sigh,
> When care is pressing you down a bit,
> Rest if you must, but don't you quit.
> Life is queer with its twists and turns,
> As every one of us sometimes learns,
> And many a failure turns about
> When he might have won had he stuck it out;
> Don't give up though the pace seems slow—
> You may succeed with another blow.
> Success is failure turned inside out—
> The silver tint of the clouds of doubt,
> And you never can tell just how close you are,
> It may be near when it seems so far;
> So stick to the fight when you're hardest hit—
> It's when things seem worst that you must not quit.[3]

Finding the right handles may often seem impossible. Anger is a complicated emotion. Paul had it. Peter had it. Jesus had it. It is legitimate to have it. But what do we do with it after we have it? Find the handles, even though slowly. Don't give up until you have them. They are there somewhere waiting for us to dig them out.

What power there is in Ephesians 4:26-28, " 'In your anger do not sin:' Do not let the sun go down while you are still angry, and do not give the devil a foothold. He who has been stealing must steal no longer, but must work, doing something useful with his own hands, that he may have something, to share with those in need" (NIV). Paul was prescribing a formula for burnout that results from anger. Don't get stuck with it. Don't be fooled by it. Don't prolong it. Don't deny it. Work on it. Work through it. With God's help and with the active grace in our relationships we can live with the feelings which are ours as human beings and live redemptively.

7

Burnout Is an Authority Problem

We have heard the words said or implied almost daily. "Nobody is going to tell me what to do." Inherent in every thinking and creative person is the desire to be free. Freedom is one of the most obvious of God-given traits. Instinctively, we want to be a part of a free society. When authority is present, freedom is a necessary part of the plot. Freedom must be defined in the face of authority.

Wars have been fought in every century over the rights of freedom. Economy, society, values, and religion, are determined in large measure by the concept of authority.

Even in the heart of the Christian faith, at the very beginning, is the concept of authority. "And God spoke all these words: 'I am the Lord your God, who brought you out of Egypt, out of the land of slavery. You shall have no other gods before me" (Ex. 20:1-3, NIV). Authority is at the heart of life. When authority is established, all men reckon with their own freedom as they respond. It is natural.

Those persons who have not dealt with the problem of authority in their own lives will have the most problems with burnout. Those ministers who have a built in resistance to structure will chafe more in the years where burnout is a possibility.

INNER STRENGTH

The new birth gives us inner strength. Prior to the new birth, God developed us uniquely in order to be used in his purpose. The new birth then frees us to do what God intended for us to do. Understanding this releases us from the need to prove ourselves.

In its simplest form, inner strength is the freedom from having to prove ourselves. Those leaders who have to spend much of their energy proving their worth deplete their strength. Inner strength, for the

Christian, is dependence on God. It is the recognition of something greater than ourselves.

Fear is the culprit. Fear keeps us from finding the inner strength that is necessary for resolving the authority problem. We are afraid of being done in. We are afraid of being ignored. We are afraid of being squeezed out. We are afraid we will not be recognized. These and other fears keep us from finding inner strength.

Our heritage and environment do a great deal to us. Depending on how we respond, our parents create an atmosphere for us where fear can be prevalent. Or they create for us an atmosphere where we are virtually free from fear. Many behaviorists believe that the study of authority in personality structure can be best understood in the study of the relationships to parents. If, for example, our parents were affirming, supportive, and understanding, we are more apt to feel positively toward authority. If, on the other hand, our parents were judicial, harsh in discipline, and highly disapproving of mistakes, we are more apt to feel cautious toward authority. We may even feel suspicious toward authority.

It is not that simple. Understanding our past is helpful. It is not the catchall for understanding the fear of authority or the freedom from fear of authority. Having had loving parents does create for us a better foundation for inner strength.

Fear can be nourished. If the most predominant feeling in our relationship to authority is fear, then it is obvious that the structure will always give us trouble. We cannot relax. We nourish it and it grows.

The antithesis to fear is love. The resource for inner strength is God's love for us. Without it we will fear. We will build a monster in every authority relationship. But with God's love we can find inner strength. It is not so easy. Those who preach God's love as if all you have to do is relax and it will come have had different experiences than I. I have had to build my own trust system in believing in God's love. In 1 John 4:18, there is a passage which will help in building our inner strength. "Love is made complete among us so that we will have confidence on the day of judgment, because in this world we are like him. There is no fear in love. But perfect love drives out fear, because fear has to do with punishment. The man who fears is not made perfect in love" (1 John 4:17-18, NIV). "Drives out" suggests a process, not a simple happening.

If authority represents punishment when we make mistakes, we will fear. We will deny our system of inner strength. But if authority represents direction, we are in a position to drive out fear.

PAYING THE RENT

Learning to live with a healthy outlook on authority is another way of "paying the rent." If you pay the rent you are free then to do what you wish with the rest of your time. But if paying the rent is a barrier, discontent cannot be far behind.

Philosophically, the Church Administration Department of the Baptist Sunday School Board has done much in trying to restore the "servant" role of the deacon. Realistically, we know that the power structure in a Baptist church still resides within the deacon body. It is as it should be. Deacons are servants, it is true. But deacons are also those who are relied upon to make decisions. At least they are relied upon to influence decisions. One of the words we use a great deal is "legitimizers." The deacons in most Baptist churches are "legitimizers" in making the most far reaching decisions. Some pastors have picked up the "servant" role of the deacon in an effort to dilute some of their power. They have stressed much of the ministry of the deacon in an effort to centralize the authority more in other areas. Perhaps they wish to centralize the authority in their own behalf. They (the pastors) discourage the "legitimizer" role of the deacon. They try to shift the power.

Philosophically, I agree with where the Church Administration Department has stood for the past twenty-five years. We do emphasize the role of the deacon as servant. He should be more involved in the spiritual welfare of the church. However, when pragmatism raises its head, we know that deacons are still the basic power structure in most Baptist churches.

The pastor has a choice. He can choose "not" to pay the rent. He can choose to relate to the deacons as if they were not part of the power structure over the past generations. He can idealize himself into believing that he does not have to recognize their influence in a decision as big as building a family life center. Or he can "pay the rent." He can work through all the formal and informal structures of authority and do his work more effectively.

The point is, "paying the rent" is a recognition of authority where it really is. It may be with the deacons. It may be with the church council. It may be with the church staff. It is still the recognition of where it actually is and learning to live with it in an effective and redemptive way.

Paul spoke of authority in his letter to the church at Rome. He wrote, "Everyone must submit himself to the governing authorities, for there is no authority except that which God has established. The authorities that exist have been established by God. Consequently, he who rebels against the authority is rebelling against what God has instituted, and those who do so will bring judgment on themselves" (Rom. 13:1-2, NIV). It is true that we must interpret these verses in the context for which they were intended. The zealots were impatient. There were still Christians who felt that the way to establish Christianity was through the political strength of the existing government. The kingdom of God is not built on overpowering people militarily and politically. The kingdom of God is built on the love which is in Christ. "Do not repay anyone evil for evil. Be careful to do what is right in the eyes of everybody. If it is possible, as far as it depends on you, live at peace with everyone. Do not take revenge, my friends" (12:17-19a, NIV).

MEASURING THE TURF

Where does my turf begin? Where does it end? Where is my playing field? Who is the coach? A minister wants to know where he can go and feel like he has some authority. He wants to know where his turf ends. He wants to know how far he can go even when he is not in charge.

A pastor sat in a deacon's meeting describing his vacation plans. He was aware of the fact that the church had not budgeted for the supply preacher while he was gone. The pastor and the deacons were discussing some of the options. The pastor had willingly offered to pay the supply while he was on vacation.

One deacon suggested, "Why don't you just go on your vacation, and let us handle it?" As the minister was telling the story, he confessed that he did not know why the statement was so threatening to him. He had always felt that the pulpit was his domain. That was his turf. All of a sudden, his turf was no longer his turf. He felt the deacon was infringing on his own territory. Since it was the first time that his turf had been challenged, the pastor almost decided against going on vacation. Fortunately, he went ahead and negotiated with the deacons themselves to fill the pulpit for him. He had suggested the procedure and thus was much more comfortable with this approach.

Measuring the turf is only part of the solution to this thorny problem. Protecting the turf is still another facet. He must feel secure enough to allow others c . . turf. He must be adept at giving his turf away while still maintaining the control. It is often like walking a tight wire in a carnival act.

One church I pastored was full of ordained ministers. I was pastor in a college town and the college community was a large part of the membership. Each Sunday I preached to more than a dozen who had seminary training. Most had doctorates which was even more intimidating. It was inevitable that I should have a turf problem. More specifically, it was inevitable that I should have an authority problem.

We were writing a church constitution and bylaws. We discussed those areas of theology and doctrine that I felt comfortable in discussing. However, most of the adult membership felt comfortable, as well. One particular member was extremely bright. He had a highly responsible position on the teaching faculty. After two or three meetings with the committee writing the church consititution and bylaws, I found myself more defensive than I should be. I found myself protecting every opinion I was expressing. I was especially protective with this particular person.

I stored it up. Finally, when he suggested that a huge chunk of the newly written proposal (written by me) be deleted, it was the proverbial straw. I remember the words I spoke because they sounded like they came from someone else, "If you had written that statement you would have said the same thing, but you would have been satisfied with it. Since it came from me, you are having real trouble with it, aren't you?"

There was deathly silence. I asked myself, *Who was that that spoke?* It could not have been me. I would never have acted so childishly. Yet, they were all staring at me as if I were the one who had spoken. I was embarrassed. I did not get out of the situation smoothly. It was awkward for all of us.

As I was relating this humiliating experience to my friend and counselor, Dr. Everett Barnard, I was still trying to protect my turf. After all, this was my area of expertise. I was the pastor of the church. Why was he challenging my authority? Why was he so hardheaded?

Everett listened sympathetically, then he asked, "Who was he, Brooks?"

"What do you mean, Everett? I have already told you who he was," I suggested.

"No, he is someone else to you. Who was he?"

I was stunned. I did not know how to respond. Everett did not help me either. He let the silence take its toll. Eventually, it hit me. He was my brother. My older brother always succeeded economically. He was seventeen years older than I and he had experienced the world. The professor was also about sixteen to eighteen years older than I. My brother always knew more about life than I did. He had so much more influence on my Dad than I, and it bothered me. I wanted to be more influential with Dad. I was not happy with the favorite son role. I wanted the older brother role. I had encountered an authority problem in the church constitution and bylaws committee. He had infringed on my turf, and it made me angry. I was not so certain why it made me angry until Everett helped me to know.

It may not be true for you. It is true for me. I have found that almost every time that a matter of turf is in question, I have to go back and landscape my familial role. If I care about the people with whom I live and work, I made of them family members first. I do this before I can free them to be who they are. I forget myself from one group to the next. My dad is almost always in the congregation. My mother is there. My two brothers and my three sisters are there. I go through the feelings of family with them, and hopefully with God's help I can free them in my own prejudices so that they can be who they are. If they try to usurp my turf, it takes a little longer to free them up in my own mind.

FREEING THE CHILD

An authority problem can not be solved in the minister until he has freed the child in himself. He must find the strategy for letting the child loose in an adult world.

It is the child in us that complicates the authority problem. Rather than freeing ourselves we get locked into our childish habits and make judicial and/or judgmental parents out of those with whom we work.

Every person I have known intimately has approached the parental problem differently. Sooner or later, the parent who has cared for us must be set free to be an adult. We must "leave father and mother and cleave only unto Him." We must know that the child in us yearns for escape. The child in us wants to be an adult. . . . Even wants to be parent as well. The freeing process can be very painful.

An example of the minister who has never allowed his child to find freedom from his parents is the minister who can not make a significant vocational move without consulting with, and later, getting approval from, parents.

Each time I look at Morton Rose, I see my Dad. Morton has been my friend since seminary. Certain mannerisms about him still remind me of Dad. Because of my close relationship to Dad when he was living, I am prejudiced for Morton. I must struggle to let my dad be free to be in Morton. I must find the freedom to relate to my dad in an adult manner through Morton. To do this, I must not be overly swayed by his opinions or judgment, but I must also not be fearful of the goodness which was in my dad, and that I see and feel in Morton. I must not react to his opinions and judgments as if he were trying to tell me what to do. I must be free to be independent. This process is a similar process for every significant person in my life. I must find my parents, my brothers, or my sister, and allow the freedom for them to be who they are through the people with whom I relate. I must relate to them as a child who has been freed to become an adult in a responsible world.

JUDGMENT IN AUTHORITY

Pastoral authority is nebulous. Even though it is given it must be earned. The church calls the minister and by his very office the church has given him or her the authority to exercise gifts. The minister is an

---

JUDGMENT IN AUTHORITY

1. FRIGHT
2. FLIGHT
3. FIGHT

FIGURE 7

ambassador. He or she is the representative of God. This creates three negative factors in the lives of some church members. (See Figure 7.)

(1) Fright

The first of these negative factors is fright. Some members are afraid of the judgment of pastoral authority. They are fearful of the disapproval which they feel is a possibility. Consequently, some shower gifts on the minister and do not really know why. Obviously, many shower gifts out of their love for the minister. This is a different matter altogether. But there are those who give gifts and expect some kind of favor in return. They expect some kind of recognition from the minister or they expect some kind of forgiveness. These people, in my judgment, are operating out of their "fright" of the pastoral authority inherent in the office of minister.

The minister, himself, can function out of fright for authority in the same manner as do members with him.

(2) Flight

The second of these negative factors is flight. These persons shun or avoid. They shut off the outreach of others. They shy away from intimacy. The same motivation for flight is seen in the first mentioned above, fright. The judgment is a fearful addendum to any part of the relationship. These persons fear being disapproved of and therefore avoid persons who represent authority with a passion.

Some of the methods of flight by members are laxity in attendance, nonsupport financially or emotionally, or changing churches. The latter is for the more desperate who have identified a problem in the authority role of the minister but do not understand it well enough to work through it.

The pastor himself may respond to the judgment in authority by moving to another church.

(3) Fight

The most uncomfortable for many ministers of the three negative factors which are resultant from his role in authority is fight. Fight is conflict. It is the embroiled pain that comes from resistance to anyone who represents judgment in authority.

Lowell G. Colston in his book, *Judgment in Pastoral Counseling*, talks about the complexity of the minister as a diagnostician. As a person who diagnoses, he points to the tension between *freedom* and *determinism*. This means that the pastor, along with other members of the helping professions, "is called upon not only to distinguish the way an individual has a self-imposed disability, but also the ways in which family and community contribute to that disability."[1] If the wife of an alcoholic seeks help from the minister in his role as helper, he must also show her her own responsibility as part of the condition of the problem. She is not immune. She is also responsible. The resentment of members which comes from this role of the pastor as diagnostician often causes "fight." People who think they are totally absolved from sin and then find the minister pointing to their own responsibility are prone to fight him.

Again, in his role of pastoral authority, he passes out judgment on sin. This is his role which is given to him by God. Those who come to church and think of themselves as free from sin because they are supportive of the church find it very difficult to listen to the judgment of the prophetic role of the minister without some form of reaction. Usually this takes the form of "fight." They may fight him openly. Or they may fight him more subtly and politically. They may even fight him by working for his dismissal and/or release.

If these three negative factors are so likely from the judgment role of the minister, does the minister have the "right" of his judgment in pastoral authority?

The answer to that question is a resounding yes. The model of the authority of Jesus gives the right. George A. Buttrick wrote about this authority modeled by Jesus in *The Interpreter's Bible*.

He had the authority of *silence*. Jesus prayed and pondered. He did not cut himself off from the best wisdom of the past, but he meditated on it in silence until he became his own, in very spirit, not merely in its letter . . . He . . . spoke from sound intutition.

He had the authority of *love*. Jesus spoke from a deep fund of compassion. He healed the sick, he played with children, he had a "great heart."

He had the authority of *life*. The face of Jesus was an interpretation of his words; his deeds were of one piece with his commands. His hearers knew there were reserves of soul in him which his teaching had not tapped.

He had authority *from God*. The springs of truth in him came from a far deeper source than any human probing could find.[2]

But the minister must also turn that role of judgment around. He must look in the mirror. He himself may be fighting the battle of *fright, flight,* or *fight.* If so, he must examine the role of the deacon or church member who is giving off signals of authority from God. He must measure his own humanity and test his own skills through prayer and skillful evaluation to be sure that he is not fighting the battle in another church member that some church members are fighting toward him.

HOW TO SOLVE THE PROBLEM OF AUTHORITY

It would be glib to talk about the problem of authority and the problems it presents without talking about the prescription to the problem. The prescription sounds much more simplistic than it actually is. The solution is love through forgiveness.

Judgment in pastoral authority is not the final word. Judgment, as the pastor views authority, is not the final word. The final word is forgiveness which is in love. "For God is love; and his love was disclosed to us in this, that he sent his only Son into the world to bring us life. The love I speak of is not our love for God, but the love he showed us in sending his Son as the remedy for the defilement of our sins. If God thus loved us, dear friends, we in turn are bound to love one another" (1 John 4:9-11, NEB).

The best way to neutralize the hold a person in authority has over us is to learn how to love them. The best way to learn how to love them is to begin by forgiveness. What is there to forgive? The first part of forgiveness is to forgive yourself for feeling so put down by the authority figure. If that can be done, you can forgive the authority figure for putting you down. When those two ingredients are eliminated, you are free to love. Until they are eliminated, you are still under the bondage of feeling threatened by the authority.

As long as the authority figure bothers, there will be some kind of problem. The opposite is also true. As long as others view us as an authority figure, it causes some forms of being unapproachable. In Eric Berne's popular best seller, *Games People Play,* he asks the ultimate inevitable question, "After games, what?"[3] As long as the authority figure which distorts our vision is an obstacle, we tend to play some kind of game. We cannot be spontaneous. We cannot be trusting.

Eventually, there will be some kind of alienation. The pastor will be urged to move to another church. Or the pastor, being the authority figure, will urge others to make themselves scarce in the leadership of the church. The more vindictive minister will even encourage them to move to another church. The point is that as long as we play games, we can not solve the authority problems. We cannot improve the relationships.

CONCLUSION

Burnout is an authority problem. But an authority problem can be solved. It can be solved with the development of inner strength. The new birth in Christ gives that new inner strength. A freedom occurs which can not be explained. We are not *free from* the tyranny of others controlling us. We are *free to* find our heritage in being for God what he has called us to be.

We must pay the rent. If we are to be free to see authority as a reality with which we live, we must pay the rent of doing what we are responsible for doing. Additionally, we must measure our turf. We must know how far our limits are, and what our possibilities are.

We must free the child in us in order to respond to the parental images in a healthy way. We must learn to be adult with the freedom of the spontaneity of our child without fear of reprimand or judgment from others. We must learn to live with the judgment in our own authority as well as in the authority with which we work in the lives of church members, church leaders, and deacons. We can solve the problem of authority with the love which is Christ Jesus who teaches us how to forgive ourselves and how to forgive others.

8

Burnout and the Priorities Dilemma

Which comes first: the chicken or the egg? Winning people to Christ or growing people who will win people to Christ? The minister has no simplistic answer.

Some ministers spend all their time in personal visitation. All their high energy time, that is. When this is so, something else in their ministry suffers. Fortunately, for those who spend all their high energy time in personal visitation, there are many church members who are willing for them to do so. Unfortunately, there are many other church members who would wish for them to balance their time and balance their ministry.

Each day the minister must make deliberate decisions about his time. He has to choose priority time with planning skill. To do this he must know what is important to him. Even more, he must know what is essential to him. Where does he begin? How does he go about choosing his priorities?

PERSONS FIRST

As discussed so eloqently in the article by Daniel Yankelovich in *Psychology Today*, April 1981, the trap of self-fulfillment has been recognized by our society. We are in no-where land. After we have spent all our energy understanding ourselves, unless we have an objective to apply that understanding to the world around us, we have lost it.

People are first. Very few ministers would argue with that platitude, but it is much more than a platitude. It is good mental health.

George Burns has a new hit country record. You must, he sings, "Put people first." To do this you *love people* and *use things*. You do not *love things* and *use people*.

The complexity of our wants and needs causes us to confuse our value system. It has always confused me. How does the American mind-set work? How can we spend billions of dollars on defense (at last count we had more than 9,000 nuclear warheads to Russia's 3,000) and military space explorations, while some people living on social security can not find enough food to survive. How can we justify starvation at the expense of military strength? I believe our values are confused.

It is just as easy to get the values of ministry confused. What are we about? Are we about having the highest and the largest? Or are we about having people come to Christ and then having those same people minister to each other. Of course, they do not *have* to be contradictory. But often, it is tempting for the minister to spend more energy on the newly moved Baptist who was a faithful giver and faithful attender in another city than to spend energy with the lost persons in the community.

Leonard Griffith, in his refreshing book, *We Have This Ministry*, suggests that you can usually tell what people's priorities are by asking three

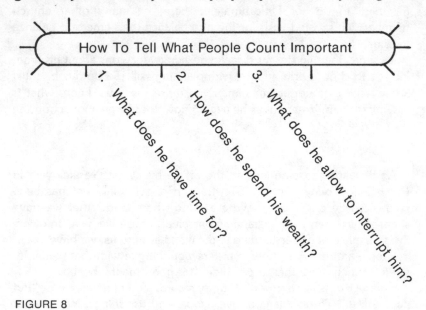

How To Tell What People Count Important

1. What does he have time for?
2. How does he spend his wealth?
3. What does he allow to interrupt him?

FIGURE 8

questions about him, "(1) What does he have time for? (2) How does he spend his wealth? and (3) What does he allow to interrupt him?"[1] (See Figure 8.)

Jesus moved with a great sense of urgency. Yet he always had time for persons. He met with one man at midnight. He met with one woman at midday. He would not let his disciples rush the children away from him. He had compassion for a wealthy, young man, it is true, but he also had time for the lame, the blind, and the sick. He spent his wealth, which was the power of God, washing his disciples' feet. He was constantly interrupted. He had someone tugging at his robe. He had a man dropped through a roof. He even stopped one of his largest gathered audiences to honor a young boy who thought to bring his lunch of fishes and loaves. The model for putting persons first is exemplified by Jesus all the way through the New Testament.

BARRIERS TO PERSONS COMING FIRST

What causes us to be blind in our priorities? We are human, but that is not an excuse. It is an explanation. Our humanity causes us to wish for less pressure from the burdens of people's pain. We want more prestige. That is a natural part of the sinful nature of man. But the desire for more recognition and prestige is one of the foibles of humanity that we must learn to cope with and we must learn to overcome.

What are the barriers to people and/or persons coming first?

(1) Preoccupation with vocation

The first barrier to persons coming first is a preoccupation with our own vocation. Knowing that we must be about God's task as a minister, many of us are prone to be so preoccupied with our own direction that we forget about what that direction is concerned with . . . persons. It is the old proverb: it is hard to see the forest for the trees. We are so busy doing things that we forget about the people with whom we should be concerned in doing those things.

The most vivid example is when Jesus was teaching and ministering to crowds of people. The disciples were concerned with the administration of the crowd. They were trying to make certain that everything "went well." They were arranging rows and groups. Some children were gathering around our Lord. The disciples saw these children as being in the way. Jesus scolded the disciples. The children are persons too, he said. These are significant people in the kingdom of God. Don't overlook them.

When the role of the prophet was described in Isaiah 61:1-3, he was describing a sacred part of what we are to do. But he was also describing a sacred part of what we are to be . . . to others.

"The Spirit of the Lord Jehovah is upon me; because Jehovah hath anointed me to preach good tidings unto the weak; he hath sent me to bind up the broken-hearted, to proclaim liberty to the captives and the opening of the prison to them that are bound; to proclaim the year of Jehovah's favor, the day of vengeance of our God; to comfort all that mourn; to appoint unto them that mourn in Zion, to give unto them a garland for ashes, the oil of joy for mourning, the garment of praise for the spirit of heaviness that they may be called trees of righteousness, the planting of Jehovah, that he may be glorified" (ASV).

Look at the key words . . .

preach
bind up the broken-hearted
proclaim liberty
proclaim God's favor
proclaim God's vengeance
comfort
joy for mourning
garment of praise

The commission to do the things that God has called us to do may cause some to become so preoccupied with the sense of their own importance that we forget completely that the reason for the commission is to reach and teach the lost.

The preoccupation with our own vocation must never become so strong that we lose sight of the needs of others. We must continue to work to be empathic to the hurts and pains of those who hear us as we proclaim and comfort.

(2) Unwillingness to let the bird fly

There is an old proverb: Give the bird room to fly. The reason why it is so difficult for the minister to let the bird fly is that it is so reassuring to have the bird dependent. To have the congregation emotionally dependent upon us reaffirms our own sense of importance.

It is also a preoccupation with our needs and not the needs of those to whom we minister. We are more concerned with getting things done than in growing people when we are more comfortable having them rely upon our judgment more than on their own.

(3) Unwillingness to give them room to make mistakes

It is hard to turn them loose . . . to release them. That is the heart of letting the bird fly. It is even harder to overcome the temptation to snatch them up and bring them back into our own nest when they make mistakes.

There seems to be as much or more compassion in the desire to want to keep church members from making mistakes than in turning them loose in the first place. Simply to let the bird fly shows our own need for security. To want to snatch them up and protect them seems to be more caring . . . but it is more "smothering." We must give them enough room to make mistakes but then affirm them in spite of their mistakes.

(4) Dissipated energies

One of the best indications of dissipating energies is in trying to touch "everyone" with our ministry and neglecting the "someones." With all that Jesus was commissioned to do while he was on earth, why did he spend so much time with so few? He concentrated a large proportion of his ministry to just a comparatively few people. Was it poor planning? No. It was the purposeful will of God to prepare the few to reach the many.

It is tempting to want to spread ourselves so thinly that we avoid the real task at hand. We can more easily concentrate our energies on those who are willing for us to minister to them.

Judas felt Jesus was mismanaging his brief ministry. Judas wanted Jesus to establish himself as a political superstar. The rock opera, *Jesus Christ Superstar*, has Judas cry into the face of the mob, "Everytime I look at you I don't understand."[2] He wanted more than Jesus was intending to do with his life. He felt Jesus' timing was bad. He could overthrow the political system with his powers. Judas' betrayal was much more than a simple whining greed for thirty pieces of silver. He wanted his own needs satisfied. But Jesus was content to spend his time with the people. He was happy being with his disciples. The crowds flocked to Jesus. He did not use mass communication and sophisticated public relations techniques to draw the crowds. Jesus concentrated his energies on those who would carry out the Great Commission after he was crucified.

It is easy to become so intensely concerned with managing our energies to avoid the cries of Judas that we overlook the redemptive work of the time well-spent with the few.

(5) The need to please

Many well-intentioned church members have super expectations of their minister. They want him to be the central figure of the community. They want him to be a preacher equal to Billy Graham. They want him to visit at extraordinary hours. We did a survey at our conference centers at Glorieta and Ridgecrest in 1978 on what people expect of their minister. We divided the areas of the life of the minister into several specific phases. We showed the number of hours in the week, 168. Eight (8) percent of the people who participated in the survey expected more than 200 hours of work for the minister in a week.

The need to please *some* has caused a great deal of neglect to *many*. I will call him Clarence. He was so hard to please that I thought I would build a deliberate strategy to see if I could make him like me. I did, but it took six months. The folly of my strategy was that I could have divided that energy so that there were many others who could have been "pleased" and my ministry would also have been much more effective. I was used by my own compulsive need to please.

These are but five of the barriers to putting persons first. If you make a list, you will come up with three or four times that many. The bottom line is, reach back into your reservoir of commitment and put the needs of persons back into proper perspective.

A PLAN TO REESTABLISH PRIORITIES

According to a fable an eel who was trying to make his way across the Atlantic Ocean. After seeking directions from several other sea creatures who themselves did not know where they were going, a crafty shark, pointing to his open mouth, said, "This is the way!" The eel swims in, trusting the directions of the shark. The last line of the fable is,

"If you do not know where you are going, you will end up someplace else."

This can happen to the minister. If he doesn't know where he is going, he is sure to end up someplace else. He will end up with the frustration and the futility that comes from not having his priorities straight. Some practical suggestions can help reestablish priorities.

(1) Rebuild the center

If you had to draw your life into one word, what would that one word be? Paul spoke of Christ as "before all things, and in Him all things hold together" (Col. 1:17, NASB). It is easy to say that our lives are built around "Christ," but very difficult to maintain that discipline. We want our lives to reflect the model of Christ, but the temptations of sin are ever present.

The minister must first of all be a Christian. He must display his Christian principles as a representative of who and what he is about. Without that center, he is aimless, and will certainly burnout before he reaches middle age. He will find his priorities divided against themselves and he will lose his purpose for being. He will find other vocations of more interest and appeal.

Ernest Mosley suggested in his book, *Priorities in Ministry* that there are certain dynamics to meeting the challenge for centering our person-hood on Christ. In Galatians 5:22-23, "the fruit of the spirit is love, joy, peace, patience, kindness, goodness, faithfulness, gentleness, self-control" (RSV). Mosley develops these into the specific patterns for centering our faith as a Christian person into renewed priorities.

"He should be a loving person"[3] Love is the ability to recognize Christ in others and relate to them accordingly.

". . . a joyful person."[4] Joy is being so full of the purpose and being of Christ that it is exciting to be alive. It is the ability to see purpose even in pain and hurt.

"He should be a peaceful person."[5] Peace is the power to experience setback without embracing futility. Peace is reaching for stability that only comes in the Spirit of God. "Peace I leave with you; my peace I give to you; not as the world gives do I give to you" (John 14:27, RSV).

". . . A Patient Person."[6] Patience is the hope of having things happen without the panic of needing to make them happen.

". . . A Kind and Good Person."[7] Kindness and goodness may best be described as the absence of vindictiveness and unwarranted judgment. It is the generosity toward the imperfect humanity of others.

". . . A Faithful Person."[8] In the original Greek language, the word *pistis*, is the same word for "faith" and "belief." To be a faithful person is to be a believing person. One who is faithful believes that God is the Creator and Redeemer of all mankind. A faithful person has integrity. He is not divided against himself. He does not show one side of himself to his church and another side of himself to his wife and family. He is the same. He does not put on a mask to be seen by others in order to impress them that he is faithful. He is faithful and is consistent.

". . . A Tolerant Person.[9] Tolerant means one does not take undue offense. He is not bent on blaming the world for what ails him. He can weather the storm. He can bend with the wind as a willow that gives but moves back to its former shape after the strong wind.

". . . A Self-Controlled Person."[10] Self-control is the ability to avoid fragmentation. It is the ability to deal with the danger of going to pieces and then putting the pieces back together again.

(2) Discipline your time

A plan to reestablish your priorities is self-control. It is also the self-discipline. But what exactly is self-control and self-discipline without the ability to manage time? The second phase of reestablishing priorities is learning to manage the precious commodity, time.

Paul wrote, "I tell you, now is the time of God's favor, now is the day of salvation" (2 Cor. 6:2*b*, NIV). Each person has 168 hours per week. Each person has 24 hours per day, 60 minutes per hour. "I don't have time!" is not a legitimate statement. Everyone has exactly the same amount of time. Using time wisely is the important ingredient in establishing priorities.

a. *Time wasters* (See Figure 9.)

To discipline your time you need to know what is wasting your time.

Inefficiency. A job done poorly is a monstrous thief of time. If you don't have time to do it right, when will it ever be done right? Do it efficiently the first time and take a little longer. You will save time.

Indecision. This may be another part of the real monster, "procrastination." Procrastination is often indecision because the decision is unpleasant, distasteful, or time consuming.

TIME WASTERS

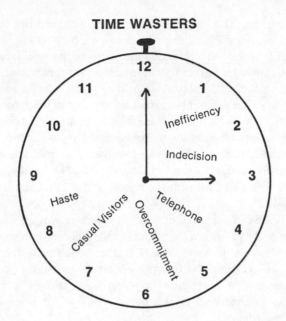

FIGURE 9

Telephone. One of the biggest excuses for not studying is the telephone. Many use the telephone frequently because they feel it is more pleasant than the discipline of study. The rationalization is that we "care" about people. But in reality, most telephone callers are looking for the same thing we are looking for: diversion away from the mundane. We can use our office staff more. Or, if we do not have an office staff, we can be more gently direct. In the long run, we will win the respect of our members much more than if we allow them to constantly interrupt. This, of course, does not apply to emergencies, and real areas of need. These are times when the minister must be ready to be interrupted.

Overcommitment. Broad interests cause many good and effective ministers to become overcommitted. It causes confusion in priorities and a failure to set priorities. Learning to say *no* may be the most difficult thing a minister must learn to do, but it could be the most redemptive. It is redemptive in that it saves an extraordinary amount of stress on himself. It is redemptive because it teaches church members the value of time. The formula for defeating overcommitment is to learn to say *no*.

Casual visitors. The lonely and the bored need the helping compassion of the minister. But if the minister gives himself the license to be interrupted by every lonely and bored person, he will defeat his own purpose. Even Jesus had to have times alone to recuperate. Find a private place to study. Be accessible at times which have been communicated to the church members. Get others to run interference to help you with the lonely and bored members. Learn to delegate. Casual visitors are a part of the church membership. They will use you though if you allow them to do so. They must respect your rights as a person as you respect theirs. That is not too much to ask. Neither should you feel guilty for learning to deal with the casual visitor in a tactful, courteous, but brief way.

Haste. Although we could discuss hundreds of ways the minister can waste time and thus distort his priorities, we will mention one more and move on. The last is haste. Haste is impatience with detail. It is the immediate response of the urgent. Take time to get it right. Save the time of doing it over. Distinguish between the urgent and the important. Decide what is good and what is best.

   b. *Time savers*

We have talked about some of the time wasters, what about some of the time savers?

. . . . . Set a deadline for every goal. Stick to it.

. . . . . Don't trust your memory. Carry a pencil and paper and jot things down.

. . . . . Work through small committees. Don't involve more people than is necessary. The more people involved, the more there will be need for extraneous sifting, sorting, and analyzing.

. . . . . Be clear when you are delegating.

. . . . . Again . . . . . learn to say no and stick to it. Don't get stuck with doing things just to be obliging. Especially don't get stuck with doing things just because you do not want to upset the system.

. . . . . Learn to use the wastebasket. Working for a large Christian publishing house which communicates to Christian leaders by mail, I know how dangerous it is to say that. It is true nevertheless. You must learn what to throw away and then do it.

. . . . . Find your energy spots. Some parts of the day are more productive than others. Use your energy spots to do your more complicated and heavy work. You will save enormous amounts of time if you can identify what those energy spots are.

. . . . . Plan your time alone. Just as important to finding your energy spots is planning your time alone. Recuperative time may be one way of expressing it. Reflecting time may be another way of expressing it. I choose to call it "processing" time. Most of my best ideas have come after a discussion, or after the reading of a great and stimulating passage. Plan your time alone for processing. You will save time.

. . . . . Organize. Neatness is important. The philosophy of "a place for everything and everything in its place" is a smart one to live by.

. . . . . Make visits when people are home. I have been guilty of visiting a potential member or a lost person and at the same time hoping they were not home. I am sure I am the only one who ever did that, and I repent. But planning visits around the times when they are home will save a great deal of time.

. . . . . Train deacons to do soul-winning and hospital visitation. Permit them to represent the church. Don't try to clean up their visit. Continue the visitation only on those occasions that really call for a follow-up visit.

These are just a few ways to save time. It will help in the reestablisment of your priorities.

(3) Learn balance

Learn to balance the time spent in the order of priorities of your personhood. Mosley suggests six parts of the personhood of the minister.

> Christian person
> Employed person
> Church member person
> Parent person
> Married person
> Community person[11]

To give balance, a minister who is married should arrange time to give to his spouse and family. He should know his responsibilities as a member of the community. He should remain faithful as a church member. He should maintain his responsibilities as an employed person of the church. And, primarily, he should be a person with Christianity as his most distinguishing mark.

Herbert J. Freudenberger and Geraldine Richelson wrote a book on

Burn Out: The High Cost of High Achievement. These two authors feel that the burnout candidate is a "dynamic, charismatic, goal-oriented person."[12] They suggest that the key to finding ways to cope with the potential of burnout is to integrate the complexity of being this kind of person with the fact that high achievement is inevitable. The integration that they speak of is what I am suggesting as learning balance.

Put another way, the minister who is a burnout candidate should recognize the fact that he is not content with "business as usual." He wants more out of life than the average person. *This need to accomplish or achieve* is what brought him to the point of burnout to begin with. He needs to find the areas where he can find some satisfaction and not deny those to himself. He must not hit on three of the eight cylinders he has. He should tune his motor to run smoothly. He can not do this unless he hits on all his cylinders.

This is especially difficult for the multi talented person who has so many interests that it is frustrating to him or her. The exceptionally gifted person is more a candidate for burnout than the person who is content to have simplistic methods of operation. The multi talented person does not limit himself to a few of his life goals without frustrating himself in the life goals that are evading him.

CONCLUSION

In this chapter we have discussed the importance of having persons first. The priorities dilemma is complicated by this need. Some of the barriers to persons coming first are (1) Preoccupation with vocation; (2) an unwillingness to let the bird fly; (3) an unwillingness to give others room to make mistakes; (4) dissipated energies; and (5) the overwhelming need to please that plagues some ministers.

A plan to reestablish priorities would include (1) rebuilding the center of the Christian faith; (2) discipline of time; (3) and learning balance.

9

Refueling to Avoid Burnout

Physician, heal thyself . . .
God, our refuge

An automobile cannot run forever without refueling. A minister can not continue to be effective without refueling. If we begin with the assumption that burnout is a real problem, then we must also assume that there are ways to avoid burnout if it is worth discussing at all. There are ways to refuel.

The Greek word for "I have found it," is *euresko*. It is the same root as the word *eureka*. We all wish for the bonanza. We want it all in one quick answer. Oh, if it were only that simple! *Eureka!* But it is not. It is complex. *But* it is possible. With hard work and with intended and deliberate strategies, it is possible *to avoid burnout*. Or, if the symptoms of burnout are already there, it is possible to deal with the burnout that is already plaguing us. Perhaps with the appropriate steps and with the appropriate preparation, we, too, can witness the joy of *eureka*.

We had spent about twelve hours together in a pastoral leadership seminar. During that time, the minister had shared his autobiography. He had been averaging about eighty hours per week in his ministry. He had no nights at home during the week for himself and his family. All his conversation centered around his purpose and mission in his church. He was building a new building. His Sunday School had doubled in the past year. Yet he was having migraine headaches. He had developed an ulcer. He was having trouble sleeping at night. I asked, "What have you done for yourself lately?"

He looked at me as if I had physically hit him. He was stunned. "Don't you know," he said, "that a minister does not have the right to do anything for himself?"

"Where did you read that?"

"Doesn't everybody know that?" he asked. "The Bible teaches it! The church expects it. The whole ministry system is built around it."

Another participant spoke up. "What about treating your body as the temple of God's Holy Spirit?"

"What about Jesus' withdrawals all through the New Testament to regain his spiritual strength?" another asked.

By this time the beleaguered minister was amused at his own trap. "Jesus would have had five reporters with him when he went into the garden to pray. He would have had a group of television reporters and newsmen following him into the upper room. If he lived today, he could not have withdrawn to regain his strength."

Although the laughter was unanimous, so was the consent. Almost all the ministers gathered agreed that the pressures on the minister of today made it difficult for the minister to get away.

One minister continued. "I went on vacation last year to Myrtle Beach. We had a condominium rented for nine days. On the second day, I had a call. One of the deacons who was prominent in our church had died. Naturally, I went back for the funeral. While I was there (I had left my wife in Myrtle Beach), the widow asked me to help with the soliciting of a lawyer. The estate was sticky and the church was involved. Finally, I sent for my wife. No rest for the devoted!"

If those ministers were the exception, we could deal with it more easily. I am convinced that these are not the exception but the rule. Almost all ministers in our denomination agree that it is difficult to find room and time to refuel.

But refuel we must. If we are to avoid burnout, we must find the resources to function on. This last chapter will recommend some practical ways to refuel.

ASSUME THE ANXIETIES OF MINISTRY

The ministry is a people business. People business, by its very nature, is filled with anxiety. The ministry has its share of anxieties. We do not simply work with facts and data. We cannot do research and operate off the premise that the research is our basis of operation. We have a much more tenuous vocation. It is unpredictable. It is changing. It is disturbing. It must have its share of anxieties.

Anxiety, in its simplest form, is the foreboding feeling that something bad is about to happen. It is a threat to our security. But it is also an alarm signal. Anxiety is the way the body has of telling us that we need to do something about the circumstances around us. Since it is unpleasant most of us have some built-in devices for minimizing this emotion of anxiety.

A favorite form of built-in minimization is to try to convince ourselves that it does not exist. Spiritually, if we admit our anxiety, many of us think we are lacking. But realistically, anxiety is the God-intended and God-created manner of redirecting the body when it takes a wrong turn.

The so-called "floating anxiety" is a different matter. Floating anxiety is the feeling that something bad is certain to happen. It is not a feeling that goes away as do normal feelings of anxiety. Floating anxiety is the disturbance of the emotions to the point that it interrupts all other feelings such as joy and peace and even anger. With feelings of floating anxiety that will not leave us it is certain that we need professional help. We should see a physician quickly.

But the normal anxieties of ministry is another thing. We can learn to live with the expectation of anxiety because it is natural.

One of the seminars I attended in graduate school was in "Counseling in Severe Family Problems in the Church." Dr. Richard Bruehl, a clinical psychologist, taught the course. In addition to a great deal of wisdom in handling the nitty-gritty of sensitive counseling of family problems, Dr. Bruehl suggested that successful counseling may be as simple as "learning to deal with our own anxiety in the supportive relationship." What a burden that lifted from me. I had assumed that successful counseling was in whether or not I was able to solve the problem for the family with which I was working. Dr. Bruehl's suggestions was to lend a supportive relationship and depend on the grace of God to help the people seek out their own solution to their difficult problem. This does not mean we do not make tangible suggestions. It does. We should. But we should not carry the problem into our psyche to the point that we feel responsible for their lives. The priesthood of every believer suggests we permit room for others to solve their own problems.

INTENTIONAL COPING STRATEGIES

It is not enough to wish away our burnout syndromes. We must be active and deliberate.

(1) Professional intervention

If the manner of our coping strategies are not achieving the results we wish, then obviously we need some professional intervention. A physical examination should be the first step in professional intervention. Often the help needed can be as simple as following the prescribed suggestions of a physician.

If the coping strategy is more serious, then we should not allow our pride to keep us from attaining the professional help we need. There are a number of ways to get this additional professional intervention with a minimum of difficulty.

a. Get the physician to recommend a counselor—either a psychiatrist (if the burnout symptoms are severe), or a clinical psychologist. Note the symptoms carefully. If you are losing sleep consistently, and you have no apparent reason, you probably need some outside professional intervention. If your moods are extremely irregular, you also need to consider getting some help. If the mood is acute depression, do not hesitate to get help.

b. Most hospitals of denominational orientation have some form of counseling procedure which is adjusted and attuned to the needs (both financial and psychological) of ministers. Check with the chaplain. He will be able to direct you to some help.

c. Our Baptist seminaries have pastoral care programs which have met the needs of many ministers. Trained counselors will assist in setting up a counseling program to help.

d. The Baptist Sunday School Board has a program which has helped ministers for the past decade. The Career Guidance Section offers a number of programs designed to help ministers who are having trouble coping with the problems and turmoil brought on by the vocation of ministry. The Personal and Professional Growth Course is an eleven day program conducted in Nashville and on the campuses of some of our seminaries. The program is designed to identify the specific trouble spots in the behavior and in the daily routine of ministry. The practical approach of the Course is designed to give the minister a feedback system with his peers to look at his own skills in a nonthreatening environment. Contact the Career Guidance Section at The Sunday School Board, 127 Ninth Avenue, North, Nashville, Tennessee 37234, for information.

Additionally, the Career Guidance Section offers a Career Assessment program which is three days in length. It is especially designed for individual attention. Usually the program is designed to include the spouse.

(2) Peer intervention

Many colleagues can help if permitted to do so. It is possible to attain practical help from peers with whom you communicate and associate if pride does not prevent.

Check the symptoms to see if your peers can help. If you have begun to detach yourself with your language you may need attention. For example, if you have begun to become more and more impersonal in your conversation it could mean some precautions need to be taken. If judgment language creeps into your conversation you may need to check it out with your peers. An example of judgment language is "Mr. Haroldson is neurotic. Mrs. Jones is a bickerer. The congregation is not fair to me."

Another way of detaching ourselves even before we know that we have is to become cynical. We take one step beyond being judgmental as discussed above. We become negative in our entire attitude toward people. We find ourselves reliving conversations with persons who are in our churches and wishing we had said more than we said in order to put them down. The cynicism which overcomes us is a dangerous symptom of burnout and should be checked periodically for prevention.

Our peers can help us to know that our conversation has become judgmental or that our attitude has become cynical. Check them out with the persons who have received our trust.

(3) Self-intervention

The first of the interventions discussed above was professional. The second of the interventions was peer intervention. The third is simply self-intervention.

John D. Adams has written a very helpful and practical book on *Understanding and Managing Stress . . . A Workbook in Changing Life Styles.* One of the most interesting suggestions was "self-healing.[1] He does not suggest that the self is more capable of healing than is divine intervention, but he does suggest that the equipment for self-healing is given for our own help by the Creator. He suggests the basic components of self-healing are as follows,

- Motivation, or an earnest desire to effect a change;
- Relaxation, achieved through use of the progressive relaxation technique; (we will discuss momentarily)
- Concentration on limiting the scope of the goal!
- Direction of innate energies by visualizing the desired results.[2]

The progressive relaxation technique is composed of getting the body completely comfortable. By doing this, we must find the position that is most comfortable for us. It may vary from one person to the next. We must close our eyes and concentrate on breathing easily. Then we must instruct all our bones and muscles, one at a time to relax. It is suggested that we begin at the feet and work up to the head. For example, we may start with the feet, then move to the ankles, lower legs, knees, upper legs, and hips, backbone, neck, then the top of our head.

We should do the same thing with our hands, wrists, lower arms, elbows, upper arms, neck, and shoulders.

The key is to focus on each part of the body and instruct the body to relax. With the concentration the relaxation is much more possible. The head muscles should be given separate attention. The jaws, face, and scalp are essential in the relaxation process to complete the relaxation response.

Additional attention should be given to the breathing rate. It should be slowed in order to induce the appropriate response. Then concentrate on the heart beat. Concentrate on complete relaxation at whatever heart beat is comfortable for you.

This exercise should take about fifteen or twenty minutes. For best results, it should be done at least twice each day during the time that stress is affecting burnout.[3]

For the progressive relaxation technique, a quiet setting is essential. No distractions should be allowed. A passive attitude is best. A comfortable position is mandatory.

(4) Divine intervention

Certainly the most essential intervention for taking deliberate strategies to avoid burnout is divine intervention.

a. Meaningful prayer

Find a private place. Take whatever is necessary to get the consciousness of the presence of God.

An example is to read aloud Psalm 24, "The earth is Jehovah's, and the fulness thereof, The world, and they that dwell therein. For he hath founded it upon the seas, And established it upon the floods. Who shall ascend into the hill of Jehovah? And who shall stand in his holy place? He that hath clean hands and a pure heart, Who hath not lifted up his soul unto falsehood, And hath not sworn deceitfully. He shall receive a blessing from Jehovah" (vv. 1-5a, ASV).

Concentrate on your own needs. Identify them aloud to God. Trust him to help you deal with them. Read the Scripture passage again. Remind yourself of the promises of God, and glory of his majesty. Remind yourself of the comfort of his presence.

b. Look for the intervention of God

Look for the intervention of God in the *expected* places. The worship experiences in church are one of the expected places. Acknowledge his presence. Know that he is there. Expect him to answer your prayers for the intervention of your met needs.

Look for the intervention of God in the *unexpected* places. . . . In the comments of a child. . . . In the response of a spouse. Look for the intervention of God in places where you would not ordinarily look.

c. Remind yourself of the promises of God

Read aloud the passages which are examples of the promises of God. For example:

Let not your heart be troubled: believe in God, believe also in me. In my Father's house are many mansions; if it were not so, I would have told you; for I go to prepare a place for you (John 14:1-2, ASV).

And he that searcheth the hearts knoweth what is the mind of the Spirit, because he maketh intercession for the saints according to the will of God. And we know that to them that love God all things work together for good, even to them that are called according to his purpose (Rom. 8:27-28, ASV).

For we know that if the earthly house of our tabernacle be dissolved, we have a building from God, a house not made with hands, eternal, in the heavens (2 Cor. 5:1, ASV).

For by grace have ye been saved through faith; and that not of yourselves, it is the gift of God; not of works, that no man should glory. For we are his workmanship, created in Christ Jesus for good works, which God afore prepared that we should walk in them (Eph. 2:8-10, ASV).

Read these promises aloud. Keep yourself reminded of the promises of God. God is intervening in our lives to take care of our needs. We must not become so callous and familiar with the promises of God that we lose their majesty and grandeur for our own lives.

DEVELOP A COPING CHECKLIST

Develop a checklist which helps to cope with stressors on the job and at home and then administer the appropriate prescriptions to dealing with the stressors.

The following is the Faulkner Checklist. These are a list of the things which I must contend with if I am to be a reasonable person with the people that are important in my life.

FAULKNER CHECKLIST

1. Am I acknowledging my own limitations? _____
2. Am I acknowledging my own assets? _____
3. To other people, do I treat them with care? _____
4. Am I punctual with appointments? _____
5. Under pressure, do I take extra time to make sure I have all the facts before making an important decision? _____
6. Can I play golf without feeling guilty about other equally important immediate concerns? _____
7. Is my reading balanced or simply work related? _____
8. Do I take deliberate pains to broaden my interests? _____
9. Do I feel comfortable working with people who are unlike me? _____
10. Do I enjoy meeting and talking with people who have different ways of looking at the world? _____
11. Do I get upset when things don't go my way? _____
12. When I am blocked in a decision, can I consider the options without undue frustration? _____
13. Do I get bored easily? _____
14. Do I find myself getting insensitive to the sacred? _____
15. Can I stop long enough to pat a dog? _____
16. Does my wife and family consider me as always on the go? _____
17. Is love more than a word in my vocabulary? _____
18. Do I appear disagreeable to those who work for me? _____
19. Do I appear disapproving to those for whom I work? _____
20. On the job do I often "bite off more than I can chew?" _____
21. Do I take time to be considerate? _____ tactful? _____ courteous? _____
22. Has God been personal to me today? _____

23. Have I shared my faith through my relationships? _____
24. Have I made a new friend within the past month? _____
25. Do I remember the proverb, "It is not the last blow of the ax that fells the tree?" _____
26. Do I find myself gravitating to the things in my work that are more comfortable? _____

These are but a few of the things which are important in my life for coping with the stresses which lead to burnout. Yours will be different. You will need to develop your own. These have been helpful to me. I am indebted to Alan A. McLean, and his book, *Work Stress,* for help in the development of my own checklist. (See previous discussion on "How to Turn Anger into Compassion" for reference to this work.)

See also John D. Adams, *Understanding and Managing Stress,* for a further discussion on how to cope with stress.

The Ministers Life and Casualty Union, has an excellent pamphlet, entitled, "Nobody's Perfect," which is free for the asking. The address is The Minister's Life and Casualty Union, Ministers Life Building, Minneapolis, Minnesota 55416. They suggest nine common-sense ways to cope.

1. Learn to plan . . .
2. Accept your limits . . .
3. Have fun . . . (This may be difficult for the minister who is inclined to think that all fun is sinful. Find out what can be done for fun that is not contradictory to your moral values.)
4. Be positive about people and life . . .
5. Practice tolerance and forgiveness . . .
6. Don't compete when you don't have to . .
7. Take regular, sensible exercise . . .
8. Learn to take time for yourself . . .
9. Expose your problems to those who understand.

(This is a four-page, free pamphlet.)

DEVELOP A NETWORK OF SUPPORT

"I can get along without people," a minister told me. "I spend all of my time trying to meet their needs, and when I need my needs met I get them met best by being alone. I don't want people around when it comes to refueling for myself."

Everyone needs privacy. We can not continue without it. Those ministers who would rather be alone are usually showing the results of overexposure to people. Members feel the minister is always there to meet their needs. It is difficult for them to relate to him as if he had needs of his own. The minister above who said he could get along without people actually loves people. He is a popular pastor, and his members rely on him because they know that he loves them. But the problem is with his having to spend so much of his energies to meet their needs that he feels depleted. He needs people in a different context.

Louis McBurney knew this need. In his book, *Every Pastor Needs a Pastor,* he showed some of the reasons why the pastor becomes depleted. He needs people, but he needs the people who will not drain him of his resources. He needs a pastor himself. Who are some of these people? Who can pastor a pastor?

(1) Intimate friends

In the course of a lifetime, one develops only a very few really intimate friends. If he or she is lucky, these close and intimate friends are friends for a lifetime. These are the people who give immediate support. They do not judge. They do not disapprove. They are good listeners. They are loving and affirmative. They are trustworthy. These are the people a minister must feel comfortable in turning to when he needs the support for his own needs.

(2) Family

A wife or husband can be a best friend. Children can be people who can give support in time of need. The minister needs a supportive family. If a minister's family is draining him of his energy he hardly feels a tendency to turn to them when he himself is dragging, but the family can also be a valuable resource for support.

(3) Professional support

A minister needs a physician whom he trusts. He should have a psychiatrist and/or psychologist who is a friend. Not only does he need these professional people for the referral system in his own ministry. He needs them for the support in his own life. A physician who is a close friend can literally save the minister's life. The minister will often listen to these professional persons when he will not listen to his church or to his wife.

(4) Helping acquaintances

Not all of the helping acquaintances are close and intimate friends. But this group is as essential to ongoing and effective ministry as are the intimate friends. These are the people who give the minister general and casual feedback. These are the people who respect his professional expertise and let him know that he is respected. They give him the necessary self-esteem to function.

Recently, I finished an interim pastorate in a small town in Tennessee. Having been there only six months, I was still close enough to the members to have a painful grief experience when I left. One lady in particular followed my wife and me to the car following the last service that I conducted. As I was about to get in the car, she made a comment that has affirmed my worth for several weeks since. "You were the one God sent. Your manner of relating to people in a comfortable way was so unusual that we did not know how to accept it at first. It has made a lasting impression on all of us, but I want you to know that none has profited more from the caring spirit that you had than I. Thank you!"

The unusual part of the comment was that I had hardly said more than two or three dozen words to her, personally. She had listened and affirmed me from a distance. I had enough fuel to carry me through several days. In fact, I am still being nourished from that helping acquaintance. These kinds of surprises help us to gain support from unexpected places.

(5) Challengers

These are the people who keep us on our toes. Every church has at least one. Usually, these are the people who are themselves very faithful to the church. They are warm and affirming sorts who are rarely interruptive. They challenge the ministry by being an example themselves.

The challengers are also those who are role models for us. If we permit ourselves, we all have heroes. But many of us deny ourself this blessed privilege. Something about our American way deprives us of our heroes. We often are conned into a kind of "anti-hero" syndrome. But the role models are those who challenge us to be more than we thought we could be. They challenge us to do more than we thought we could do.

The challengers are those who energize us. They provide energy, vitality, or stimulation to us to get the maximum out of our abilities.

(6) Mentors

The mentors are those who can teach us by our trust in them. These are the persons whose opinions we respect so much that we turn to them in time of confusion and turmoil.

Mentors are those persons that are specialists in our support system. We may not turn to them often, but when we do turn to them we gain a great deal of strength and/or information that will sustain us.

One of my mentors is Kit Yeaste. Having served in the same association with him in Kentucky, I had an opportunity to learn to trust him as a fellow pastor. As the decades have passed, our trust and love for each other have grown considerably. Now, when a particularly difficult problem occurs, I know I can get affirming and wise listening and counsel from Kit. We get together infrequently, but when we do get together, it is as if we had never been apart. I could not function appropriately in my own support network without him.

(7) Educators

I struggled with this area of my network support simply because I did not know what to call it. I have decided on the simple term, educators. There are some persons and some institutions which have an ingredient which helps us to know what is going on in our field. They teach us. They stay ahead of the field to such an extent that they are the persons we turn to for learning.

An example of the educator support network is the ongoing continuing educational training we have in our particular vocation. Each year most of our seminaries conduct continuing education seminars for those who are experienced professionals. This educational portion of our support network is vital to our continuing knowledge and expertise.

Educators also add an evaluation dimension. We have an opportunity to look at our work from a distance. We can know how effective we are by comparing our work with that of other professionals. We can look at our ministry from an objective point of view and find the added help which is so necessary to fresh approaches. In turn, these help us to avoid the potential burnout.

(8) Support groups

Many of our ministers are finding support groups quite beneficial in their support network. A support group is a group of congenial persons who have found a systematic way to meet and share what is going on in their lives.

One of the most common forms of support groups is to bring four to ten persons together once or twice a month for a two to four hour period of sharing. Often the meeting has a flexible structure. Books are reviewed. Topics are discussed. Theological views are shared. Personal problems are discussed. Understanding and affirmation are quite vital to the effectiveness of support groups.

One minister in California who was a member of a support group during a difficult time in his marriage confessed that the support group actually held his family together during the most critical time because of their support and affirmation. Wives of the ministers involved in the support group got involved in the lives of the other wives and found some genuine Christian *koinonia.* I am happy to say that the minister and his wife stayed together. They are building an effective ministry in a difficult church situation.

EAT RIGHT, LIVE RIGHT

The body is the temple of the Holy Spirit. That should be incentive enough to take care of our bodies. One reason burnout is a problem to many is that these persons have not given sufficient attention to their own eating and living habits.

Good nutrition which consists of three balanced meals a day with a balance of (1) meats, (2) dairy products, (3) fruits, and (4) vegetables is an excellent beginning. Cereals and grains are vital as well. These four groups of foods ensure our obtaining sufficient vitamins, minerals, protein, and fiber. Living on sugar, caffeine, and junk foods can damage the system and cause malfunctioning of the nervous system. It can upset our ability to deal with stress thus contributing to the cancerous burnout plight.

Very few engage in a regular exercise program. Yet it is the most vital part of our body's ability to function with the day to day stress which is brought on by one continuous emotional strain after another. We are risking our health, and perhaps our job, if we do not engage in regular, nonwork activities that require sustained exertion.

A regular exercise program consists of a program of at least three times per week accelerating the heart beat to 120 or 130 for twenty or thirty minutes depending on age. One fitness expert suggests the formula, "Don't exceed your Training Pulse Rate. It's now 80 percent of 220 minus your age. That's high enough."[4] For example, if you are 50, 220x80 percent176-50 (your age) 126 pulse beat would be adequate. Some of the programs which will accomplish this are swimming, running, vigorous walking, rowing, bicycling, jumping rope, team sports, and golf (if you walk).

Any physician can help you know what your appropriate weight for your height should be. If you are more than twenty pounds overweight, you are jeopardizing your health. It not only becomes a health problem, but, in terms of role model, is suggesting to others that you do not care about your own welfare.

A PLAN OF ACTION

Develop a plan of action that works for you. This will take burnout off the drawing board and into the arena of where you live.

One that I have found helpful is,
1. I need to start . . . . .
2. I need to stop . . . . .
3. I need to improve . . . .
4. Steps I will take to change are
    (1)
    (2)
    (3)
    (4)
    (5)
5. My support network is now . . .
    (1)
    (2)
    (3)
    (4)
    (5)
6. Additional support needed is . . .
    (1)
    (2)
7. Some factors which will hinder me are . . .
    (1)
    (2)
    (3)

8. Some factors which will help me are . . .
   (1)
   (2)
   (3)
9. The risks involved in my plan of action are . . .
   (1)
   (2)
   (3)
10. To overcome these risks I will . . .
    (1)
    (2)
    (3)
11. Resources needed for my plan of action are . . .
    (1) Financial _____
    (2) Physical _____
    (3) Personal _____
    (4) Other _____
12. Some of my needs to be met are (Check those which mostly apply)
    _____ (1) Affection
    _____ (2) Duty
    _____ (3) Expertise
    _____ (4) Independence/Freedom
    _____ (5) Parenthood
    _____ (6) Husband role
    _____ (7) Security
    _____ (8) Commitment
    _____ (9) Leadership
    _____ (10) Self-assurance
    _____ (11) Trust
    _____ (12) Imagination/creativity
    _____ (13) Respect and love

CONCLUSION

The minister must find new ways of doing old and familiar things to avoid burnout. He must be inventive but he must remain true to his calling and his teachings. He must explore ways to escape excessive anxiety through fantasy which is fun and morally OK. He must not shut out vocational options but he must be true to his commitment.

He must not be deluded into thinking that changing churches will avoid burnout. He must seek the rewards of spiritual gratification in the church where he now ministers without thinking that people are different in another state. He can build new friendships and find his own needs met in being able to share Christ in a vital and real way.

He must not stop growing. If he begins to fade into the comfortable position of feeling he is able to cope with any problem because he is experienced, he is sure to burn out. If he continues to be surprised he will grow. He should look at the awesome wonder of God's creative power in the remarks of a child or a disagreeable deacon. He should look for ways to do things afresh without feeling the need to do things differently.

Notes

Chapter 1

1. Louis McBurney, *Every Pastor Needs a Pastor* (Waco: Word Books, 1977), p. 45.
2. Ibid.
3. *Young's Analytical Concordance* (Robert Young) (Grand Rapids: Wm. B. Eerdmans Publishing Co., no date listed).
4. Dag Hammarskjold, *Markings* translated by Lerf Sjoberg and W. H. Auden (New York: Alfred A. Knopf, 1965), p. 58.
5. "Satchel" Paige as quoted by Cecil G. Osborne in *Understanding Your Past—The Key to Your Future*, copyrighted © 1980; used by permission of Word Books, Publisher, Waco. Texas (p. 155).
6. Osborne, op. cit., p. 156.
7. Robert A. Raines, *Success Is a Moving Target* (Waco: Word Books, 1975), p. 28.
8. Barbara Fried, *The Middle Age Crisis* (New York: Harper and Row, 1967), p. 123.

Chapter 2

1. Lucille Lavender, *They Cry Too!* (New York: Hawthorn Books, 1976), p. 89.
2. Lavender, op. cit. p. 85.
3. Lavender, op. cit., pp. 94-95.
4. Howard J., Jr. and Charlotte H. Clinebell, *The Intimate Marriage* (New York: Harper and Row, 1970), p. 44.
5. Ibid., p. 45.
6. Clinebell, op. cit., p. 45.
7. Clinebell, op. cit., p. 46.
8. Wayne E. Oates, *The Minister's Own Mental Health* (Great Neck, NY: Channel Press, 1955), p. 164.
9. Ibid., p. 159.
10. Ibid., p. 165.

Chapter 3

1. Adapted from *Christian Herald* (Dec. 1979), p. 19. Copyright 1979 by Christian Herald Assoc., Inc. Used by permission.
2. *Executive Fitness Newsletter* (Emmaus, Pa.: Rodale Press, Inc. Feb. 21, 1981).
3. Ibid.
4. Ibid.
5. Bernard Haldane, *Career Satisfaction and Success: How to Know and Manage*

Your Strengths, Rev. Ed. (New York: AMACOM, a division of American Management Association, 1981), p. 55.

6. Haldane, op. cit., p. 55.
7. Ibid.
8. Ibid.
9. Haldane, op. cit., p. 57.
10. Haldane, op. cit., p. 58.
11. Haldane, ibid.
12. Haldane, op. cit., p. 60.

Chapter 4

1. Elizabeth O'Connor, *Search for Silence* (Waco: Word Books, 1972), p. 54.
2. Reuel Howe, *Herein Is Love* (Valley Forge: Judson Press) pp. 82 ff.

Chapter 5

1. Paul L. Warner, *Feeling Good About Feeling Bad* (Waco: Word Books, 1979), p. 22.
2. Warner, op. cit., 69.
3. Ibid., p. 70.
4. Warner, op. cit., p. 70.
5. Op. cit., p. 72.
6. Ibid., p. 77.
7. Albert Ellis, and Robert A. Harper, *A New Guide for Rational Living* (Inglewood Cliffs: Prentice-Hall).
8. Ellis and Harper, ibid.

Chapter 6

1. Daniel Yankelovich, "A World Turned Upside Down," *Psychology Today*, April 1981, p. 85.
2. Yankelovich, op. cit., p. 85.
3. Hardy R. Denham, *Living Toward a Vision* (Nashville: Broadman Press, 1980), p. 46.

Chapter 7

1. Lowell G. Colston, *Judgment in Pastoral Counseling* (Nashville: Abingdon Press, 1969), p. 172.
2. George A. Buttrick, "The Gospel According to St. Matthew," *The Interpreter's Bible*, VII (Nashville: Abingdon Press, 1951), p. 335.
3. Eric Berne, *Games People Play* (New York: Grove Press, 1964), p. 184.

Chapter 8

1. Leonard Griffith, *We Have This Ministry* (Waco: Word Books, 1973), pp. 32-33.

2. Griffith, op. cit., p. 61.
3. Ernest E. Mosley, *Priorities in Ministry* (Nashville: Convention Press, 1978), p. 25.
4. Ibid.
5. Ibid.
6. Ibid.
7. Ibid.
8. Mosley, op. cit., pp. 26-35.
9. Ibid.
10. Ibid.
11. Mosley, op. cit., p. 18.
12. Herbert J. Freudenberger and Geraldine Richelson, *Burn Out* (Garden City: Doubleday, 1980), p. 39.

Chapter 9

1. John D. Adams, *Understanding and Managing Stress* (San Diego: University Associations, 1980), p. 57.
2. Adams, op. cit., 56.
3. Ibid.
4. Laurence E. Morehouse, *Total Fitness* (New York. Simon and Schuster, 1975), p. 233.